# Terror and Modernity

# Terror and Modernity

Donatella Di Cesare

Translated by Murtha Baca

polity

First published in Italian as *Terrore e modernità* © Giulio Einaudi editore s.p.a, Turin, 2017

This English edition © Polity Press, 2019

Polity Press
65 Bridge Street
Cambridge CB2 1UR, UK

Polity Press
101 Station Landing
Suite 300
Medford, MA 02155, USA

ISBN-13: 978-1-5095-3148-6
ISBN-13: 978-1-5095-3149-3 (pb)

A catalogue record for this book is available from the British Library.

Library of Congress Cataloging-in-Publication Data

Names: Di Cesare, Donatella, author.
Title: Terror and modernity / Donatella Di Cesare.
Other titles: Terrore e modernità. English
Description: Cambridge, UK : Polity Press, 2019. | Includes
    bibliographical references and index. |
Identifiers: LCCN 2018049242 (print) | LCCN 2018051323 (ebook) |
    ISBN 9781509531516 (Epub) | ISBN 9781509531486 | ISBN
    9781509531486q(hardback) | ISBN 9781509531493q(pbk.)
Subjects: LCSH: Terrorism. | Terrorism–Religious aspects–Islam. |
    State, The.
Classification: LCC HV6431 (ebook) | LCC HV6431 .D52416 2019
    (print) | DDC 303.6/25–dc23
LC record available at https://lccn.loc.gov/2018049242

Typeset in 10.5 on 12 pt Sabon
by Toppan Best-set Premedia Limited
Printed and bound in Great Britain by TJ International Limited

For further information on Polity, visit our website:
politybooks.com

# Contents

## 4 The New Phobocracy                               128

# 1

# Planetary Terror

No universal history leads from savagery to humanitarianism, but there is one leading from the slingshot to the megaton bomb.[1]

## 1  Bataclan

The lively shouts of students who were rushing out of the Robespierre school were dying down, while the usual background noise that marks ordinary life on the Rue Georges Tarral, a small street in the modest Parisian quarter of Bobigny, resurged. It was the afternoon of November 13, 2015. In an anonymous second-floor flat of a modern apartment block across from the school, seven men were beginning to get prepared, after having meticulously studied the plan and activated their cell phones, Kalashnikovs, and suicide vests. They were members of two commando units: one would attack the Stade de France, the other would target the open-air bistros in the 11th arrondissement, which had itself become a symbol of openness and intermingling. The members of a third group of commandos were staying in the Appart'City complex in the suburb of Alfortville, about ten kilometers from the Place de la République.

This type of operation is called "oblique" because of the strategy that was followed: organized in Syria, it was directed from Belgium. The religious mentor of the group was a 35-year-old Algerian known to French antiterrorist forces, Mohamed Belkaid. He was preparing to coordinate the attacks with a single Samsung cell phone and two subscriber identity module (SIM) cards. He would die on March 15, 2016, in Forest,[2] after having thwarted no fewer than three raids by the Belgian police, in the attempt to cover Salah Abdeslam's escape.

The three commando units spread out across Paris from one end to another were perfectly synchronized. Nothing was left to chance. The first attack, during a soccer match at the stadium, was intended to divert attention; the second, to draw all the resources of security forces and emergency services through a series of surprise raids, paving the way for the third, decisive attack: the massacre at the Bataclan theater. The final toll would be 130 dead and more than 360 wounded. It was the bloodiest attack on French soil since World War II. Leaving aside the devastating effects of the explosions, the men in the three commando groups fired at least six hundred rounds from their Kalashnikovs. The meteoric sequence of attacks violently imposed a battle scene reminiscent of Iraq or Syria at the heart of the metropolis. The City of Lights was plunged into the darkness of a long, bloody night. For the first time the victims were not sworn enemies; nor were they journalists or apostate Muslims, as in the *Charlie Hebdo* massacre, or Jews, as in the attack on the Hypercacher kosher supermarket at Porte de Vincennes. Global jihadism had abandoned any criterion: people were massacred indiscriminately.

The three cars used in the attacks—a Volkswagen Polo, a SEAT, and a Renault Clio—had Belgian license plates. They had been rented by Brahim and Salah Abdeslam, two French Moroccan brothers who had spent their life in Molenbeek-Saint-Jean, an overcrowded suburb of Brussels and a powder keg of radical Islam. But it cannot be said that Brahim and Salah were fervent Muslims. In 2013, after having accumulated a series of convictions for petty crimes, they opened a bar, Les Béguines, where alcohol, gambling, and drugs were the norm. Brahim, a consumer of marijuana, introverted and suggestible, was 31; he was very different from his younger brother Salah, a ladies' man who loved cars and spent his days watching ISIS videos. Both had become radicals only since the previous year, dedicating themselves to preparations for the Paris attack. Salah would be the only one to survive; after a massive manhunt he was arrested on March 18, 2016 and as of this writing he is incarcerated in the maximum-security prison of Fleury-Mérogis.

Not much is known about Mohammad al-Mahmod and Ahmad al-Mohammad, both Iraqis, who were destined to blow themselves up outside of the stadium. The same fate awaited 20-year-old Bilal Hadfi, a Belgian citizen who had enrolled the previous year in the Katībat al-Muhajirīn, the brigade of foreign fighters in Syria, where they met Abdelhamid Abaaoud and a 25-year-old French Moroccan named Chakib Akrouh. The video of Abaaoud dragging the corpses of Syrian civilians behind his off-road vehicle in the Raqqa desert had already made the rounds on the Internet. Although sought by many intelligence agencies, this Moroccan, by then 28 and carrying a Belgian passport, had managed to enter the French capital, where he was soon leading a group of nine men in a terrorist operation of unprecedented sophistication.

The three protagonists of the Bataclan massacre were all French citizens of Algerian origin. Samy Amimour, 28 years old, with a penetrating gaze and a thin mustache, was a hothead. In fact, his head would be found four hours after the attack, at the scene of the massacre, blown off by the explosion of his suicide vest. Ismaël Omar Mostefai, with his emaciated face, blue eyes, and long, scraggly beard, would have turned 30 on November 21; after a past of petty crime, he appeared in a video in the act of decapitating a hostage. At the Bataclan he fought to the end; beside him, also killed when his suicide vest exploded, was Foued Mohammed-Aggad, 23 years old, from Strasbourg. A practicing Muslim, Mohammed-Aggad shaved his armpits, a practice followed by "martyrs" before they die. This was confirmed by the coroners who performed the autopsy on his few remains. They also noted a "hyperkeratosis zone" on his forehead—a mark left by frequent prostration during prayers. The three jihadis, who had trained in the ranks of ISIS for two years, had all the determination of soldiers going into combat.

The unbroken series of attacks began at 9:17 p.m. with the first explosion. Ahmad al-Mohammad blew himself up outside Gate D of the Stade de France. Two minutes later, Mohammad al-Mahmod did the same outside Gate H. Although the shrapnel from the bombs wounded dozens of people, the casualties would have been much more serious if the attacks had taken place inside the arena. The reason why the jihadis stayed outside the stadium – a blip or part of the plan? – remains a mystery. There was a final telephone call at 9:20 p.m. between Abaaoud and Bilan Hadfi, shortly before Hadfi blew himself up.

A few minutes earlier, the SEAT in which the second group of commandos was riding had started cruising the cafés and restaurants of the 11th arrondissement—Carillon, Petit Cambodge, À la Bonne Bière... Kalashnikovs—combat weapons that are easy to procure and leave no chance of escape—were used to mow down women, men, and children, who were high-value, soft targets. The death toll came to 39. At the end of this deadly periplus, Brahim Abdeslam got out of the car and entered the small bistro Comptoir Voltaire. The images from the closed-circuit camera are grainy but Abdeslam's movements in the video are clear: he rises slowly, puts his left hand over his eyes, as if to protect them, and activates his suicide vest with his right hand.

The Bataclan, a concert venue in an orientalist architectural style that opened in 1865, got its name—originally spelled Ba-Ta-Clan—from *Ba-ta-clan*, a popular operetta or *chinoiserie musicale* composed by Jacques Offenbach. Having continued for decades as a performance venue, it offered a variety of programming, including rock concerts. On November 13 the featured act was a group from California, the Eagles of Death Metal. More than 1,500 people were packed in the orchestra pit and in the balconies, swaying to the music, dancing, taking selfies. Frontman Jessie Hughes pounded on his guitar. At 9:50 p.m. he began singing "Kiss the Devil," which starts with the lines "I'll love the devil!/I'll sing his song!" At that very moment, the first shots rang out; initially they were believed to be sound effects.

*On est parti, on commence.* This was the last message sent to Abaaoud by the third group of commandoes as they were about to enter the Bataclan theater. "We're on our way. We're starting." The first victims were gunned down on the sidewalk, outside the entrance. Inside the building, the sound of automatic weapon fire took the place of the music, marking the rhythm of the carnage for more than a half hour. From near or far, taking careful aim or firing at random into the crowd, amid cries for mercy and screams of pain, the attackers did not pause in their slaughter. Amimour and Mustafa in particular wended their way though the bodies that littered the floor, finishing off anyone who was still alive. "Why are we doing this? You bombed our brothers in Syria, in Iraq. Why did we come here? To do the same." They spoke briefly, only to justify themselves. At 10:19 p.m. they moved upstairs with a group of hostages. In the meantime, the Reuters news agency sounded the alarm. But no one could imagine the extent of the carnage. The BRI—Brigade Recherche Intervention, an elite unit of the French national police—sent special squads to the Bataclan. But there was nothing to negotiate. The jihadis only wanted to make sure that the media were present.

Barack Obama appeared on television at 11:40 p.m. to condemn "an attack not just on Paris ... an attack not just on the people of France, but ... an attack on all of humanity and the universal values that we share."[3] A few minutes later François Hollande announced a state of emergency throughout France and ordered the borders to be sealed.

It was past midnight when the BRI units launched their assault with grenades and automatic weapons. Foued Mohammad-Aggad blew himself up. A bullet reached Mostefai's heart. The macabre performance was over. Piles of corpses, tangled limbs, blood everywhere. The theater was pervaded by a deathly silence, broken only by the sound of cell phones ringing unanswered. The victims were more or less the same age as the attackers. "A few angry men have delivered their verdict with automatic gunfire. For us, it will be a life sentence." Thus wrote Antoine Leiris, who lost his young wife, Hélène Muyal, in the attack on the Bataclan.[4]

The next morning, a communiqué from ISIS appeared on YouTube: "The Islamic State claims responsibility for Friday's attacks in Paris."

## 2   War on terror

Are we at war? Many people ask this question, without finding an answer. It is as if, even on this point, all were doubt, confusion, disorientation. And yet, the day after the November 13, 2015 attacks on Paris, French authorities spoke explicitly about "war." Many western leaders took up the term, declaring "war" on the black caliphate in their turn. If on the one hand this took jurists by surprise, perplexed as they were about the possibility of recognizing ISIS as a belligerent party, on the other hand it irritated analysts, political scientists, and ordinary citizens, for whom that word carried a disturbing echo of the "war on terror" proclaimed by George W. Bush after the September 11, 2001 attacks.

We are at war and at the same time we are not at war. The grip of this contradiction brings out how difficult it is to make sense of the current epoch, which is still anchored to the bonds of peace, yet already projected toward conflict. Perhaps the new phenomenon is precisely the impossibility of distinguishing between war and peace, as if a gray zone were growing larger—a zone where traditional boundaries are blurred to the point of becoming unrecognizable. Peace and war are no longer opposites like light and darkness. And in this shadowy zone many other boundaries are in danger of disappearing. While peace appears to be increasingly illusory, war is unleashed everywhere. But what war are we talking about?

Two wars have been explicitly declared: "holy war" and "just war." On the one hand there is the attack on the West; on the other, the American military response that went into effect on October 7, 2001, with the invasion of Afghanistan, and was justified as an unending act of retribution. The "just war" gave rise to Operation Infinite Justice—the first code name of the counteroffensive, later to be replaced by the milder Operation Enduring Freedom. In both cases—the holy war, and the just war—each side imposes its own version of the conflict, and there is a foreboding that the war, be it holy or just, will never end.

The war, infinite and without boundaries, that began on September 11, 2001, at the dawn of the new century, does not contradict the "end of war" that philosophy has long posited. Indeed, for a long time war was understood as an armed conflict, motivated by a political objective, defined by rules, and itself capable of controlling and giving shape to potential chaos; the obvious conclusion to war was peace, as provisional and unstable as it might be. But this classic version of war no longer exists. The end of war no longer means the end of violence; rather, humanity has entered into a period of its history that is distinguished by "states of violence."[5] Conflict evades ritual and breaks protocols; the rule of law is shattered to bits; disorder cannot be controlled; destruction breaks down barriers and violates taboos.

The change could not be more profound. In fact it is epochal—in the sense that it marks an epoch, namely that of globalization. This is why one could speak of a "global war."[6] Of course, the term "war" seems to emphasize continuity rather than interruption. But its recurrence is inevitable in the absence of words that are capable of expressing the unprecedented condition of a world at arms, resigned never to lay them down.

Widespread, intermittent, endemic, the new global war is not an event carved into the flesh of history; rather it is a permanent state of violence, a belligerence that threatens to perpetuate itself ad infinitum, an absolute hostility, unhampered by limits, that becomes a way of life. War was supposed to be an extreme choice, a transitory exception, circumscribed in time and space; but now it is becoming a chronic process. Whatever the reasons for the innumerable conflicts throughout the world might be, war will have no end. It will never close—never come to a conclusion. The war of the new millennium, which promises to become millenary, has already englobed peace within itself—because it is a war that, in its totalizing expansion, has become one with the planet.

A decisive difference from previous war scenarios should be noted here. In order to grasp it in all its depth, we need to reconsider the relationship between war and politics. The Prussian theorist Carl von Clausewitz wrote that "war is simply a continuation of political intercourse, with the addition of other means."[7] This famous dictum sums up the way in which, in modernity, war has been seen as an ultimate tool of politics. For his part, Carl Schmitt, although he criticized

Clausewitz and pointed to the "presupposition of politics" present in war, did not depart from this modern view.[8] Proof of this is Schmitt's perplexity about gray zones and his effort to maintain stable boundaries—first and foremost between war and peace. Schmitt's entire political theory revolves around the concept of boundaries.

It was instead Martin Heidegger who cast a visionary gaze beyond modernity. In a passage in the *Black Notebooks*, he spoke of a "total war" that was neither a presupposition nor a continuation of politics; rather it seems to be a "*transformation* of politics."[9] Having emerged from the womb of politics, war was for Heidegger an excrescence that had taken the upper hand. Without being decided through a sovereign act, war constrains politics to take decisions that are as basic as they are imponderable. There are no longer winners or losers here. There is no longer room for peace, simply because war has become one with the planet and the planet has become war.

While World War II was raging, Heidegger was perhaps the only one to sense that the relationship between war and politics was being turned upside down to a point where war would imprint its seal upon that violent process of uniformization of the world that today is called globalization.

Global war, which marks a caesura with the past, is the way in which the new planetary politics manifests itself; it is the emergence of a world at arms, the epiphany of armed globalization.

This is why we should speak of a Global War I rather than a World War III. Otherwise one might believe that the current war is nothing more than a clash between worlds—between America and Islam, for example. World wars came to an end with the twentieth century—not that we didn't have enough disturbing premonitory signs, especially during World War II: for example the industrialization of war, the metallic assembly line in which soldiers were deployed like laborers, according to the rhythms of total mobilization. And we must not forget the figure of the internal enemy that the Jews represented for the Third Reich. But the geographical and ideological fronts were easily recognizable in that wartime scenario, just as the strategies and targets of the warring parties appeared to be clear. In spite of everything, politics was still managing to give shape to the world. And finally a peace was reached, no matter how unstable, and a bipolar order was achieved.

The Cold War marked the decline of modernity, its last horizon. It was difficult to imagine then that it would have been precisely the tension between the two superpowers that blocked the advent of a new, incomparably more violent epoch. The ice melting in which many saw a metaphor for a new spring caused instead increased turbulence in the stormy sea of globalization. Ten years after the dissolution of the Soviet Union, the attack on the heartland of America, the victorious superpower that had remained the epicenter of global chaos, marked the passage to the uncharted era of postmodernity. September 11, 2001 was the first dramatic revelation of the global war.

# 3   Global civil war

One might be tempted to interpret that stormy sea, its currents, and its waves according to familiar, well-established schemas. But globalization goes beyond liberal logic, Marxist criticism, negative thinking. Where definite forms and clear differences are missing, not only concepts but even metaphors risk being inadequate. Thus for example Zygmunt Bauman's well-known formula "liquid modernity" seems to be misleading, both because it suggests that the modern epoch has not come to an end and because, by emphasizing the fluid nature of reality, which is incontestable, it passes over the rigidities, resistances, and attritions that foment a potentially permanent conflict. It would be more appropriate to speak of "global disorder," but bearing in mind that chaos has different, often contradictory faces and that disorder is a plural phenomenon.

Planetary domination of technology, expansion of the capitalist economy, triumph of the market, vertiginous movement of trade, tyranny of finance, acceleration of the rhythms of production, competition, and at the same time decline of the nation-state, crisis of democracy, social unrest, ethnic contentions, wave of unprecedented migrations: globalization is all this—but not just this. Each phenomenon needs to be seen in the new context where it takes on unknown and unexpected meanings. What can be clearly seen, however, is that the inclusion of lives has also been, in great measure, an exclusion. The net has been spreading along lines of crisis, abysses in which innumerable people perish. Globalization has occurred under the banner of violent inequality. This is why it has been for some time now an armed globalization.

The new war of the globe in arms is spreading everywhere. There are no longer frontlines or frontiers. Above all, what has disappeared is the oldest and most reassuring boundary: the one between internal and external. Exteriority has dissolved. The planet is a place that no longer has external borders, while the interior is flooded with turbulent waters. This unprecedented geopolitical landscape, with its constellation of innumerable low-level conflicts, explains the characteristics of global war. Given that every point is connected with everything, even a marginal conflict at the most distant periphery could give rise to a deflagration of cosmic proportions. Any conflict is potentially global, because it catches fire in a planetary disorder that, far from containing it, in fact exacerbates it. If any place can be a frontline, it would be pointless to employ age-old war strategies such as advances and retreats. The global war is made up of attacks, reprisals, incursions, surgical bombings, high-tech operations carried out from a distance by trained technicians. It is a war of drones. The touch of a finger can blow up a city on the other side of the world. Once the frontline is dissolved, war is waged from a distance and with the aim of striking on a global scale. The theaters of war multiply and intersect. Land, sea, air: the deterritorialized war is transferred to satellites in interplanetary space. But the ominous backdrop of all of these conflicts is nuclear apocalypse—these being conflicts cloaked by delegating power, conflicts dissimulated through proxy, conflicts waged here and there in the world out of a paradoxical intention of keeping catastrophe infinitely at bay.

In earlier times, war involved two armies facing each other on battlefields outside populated centers, outside "open cities," which were not supposed to come under attack. The new global war has no regard—it explodes within cities, it strikes civilians and civilizations, it destroys skyscrapers filled with offices, cafés, supermarkets, embassies, schools, hospitals. The children lying dead beneath the rubble are considered collateral damage.

It is true that the distinction between military and civilian had already started to disappear as early as World War I. No fewer than 62 million civilians were killed in conflicts of the twentieth century. But the peculiarity of global war, which is situated at the end of this process, resides in the growing privatization of war. As the monopoly on legitimate violence is increasingly taken away from nations, civilians are not just helpless victims—they are also protagonists. Suffice it to think of jihadi militants, Kurdish *peshmerga*, or independent philo-Russians, for example.

In a note added to *War and Peace*, Tolstoy mocked the pretensions of those who thought that they could discover the causes of war. This applies all the more to an infinite and boundless war that, properly speaking, has neither beginning nor scope. It is impossible to say that globalization is the cause that has unleashed it. Nor does it make sense to trace it back to a chain of causes. It is rather as if this intermittent war took concrete shape here and there for the most diverse reasons, which often pile up—from control over oil to control over water, from famine to ethnic violence. Globalization is the frame in which the latent potential of each individual conflict comes to light.

Global war, which has gained the upper hand over politics, leaving behind the duel between nations, no longer depends upon the sovereign decisions of nations. It imposes itself—to such an extent that it ends up looking like a natural phenomenon. The exception becomes the rule, the extreme takes an established place among daily occurrences.

If the internal and the external dissolve into each other in a geopolitical landscape characterized by outbursts of hostility and animated by outpourings of rage, the global war has yet to reveal its most horrifically savage aspect: that of civil war. But in this case as well, the form that emerges is not the traditional one. This is not merely the case of a fratricidal war within the boundaries of a single nation. Within the global frame, civil war takes on particular contours.

It was not by chance that, independently of each other, both Carl Schmitt and Hannah Arendt introduced the concept of a "worldwide civil war" for the first time in 1963. Schmitt alluded to it in his *Theory of the Partisan*, where he spoke of a new world order, a "*nomos* of the earth" in which mutual recognition between sovereign nations would fail and war would criminalize the enemy to the point of instigating his annihilation.[10] For her part, Arendt, in her book *On Revolution*, briefly examined "the civil discord that tormented the Greek *polis*"; but in the end she left the topic in the dark.[11]

Perhaps this is one of the reasons why there is still no doctrine of civil war, a phenomenon that is at least as old as democracy. This absence is all the more glaring if we consider the proliferation of conflicts that are no longer "international" but have been defined as "internal wars" or "uncivil wars." In reality such wars seem to be aimed not at transforming the political system but rather at making disorder more acute and widespread. While the need to manage conflict has been affirmed, the question of civil war has instead been neglected.

Giorgio Agamben has dedicated a short book to this theme—*Stasis: Civil War as a Political Paradigm*. The word *stasis* in the title is the ancient Greek term. Philosophers were very familiar with civil war. Plato dwelled in several places on that singular conflict, which had divided the citizens of Athens—a "family" war in which brother killed brother. In the classical Greek world, *stasis* was the bloody discord that always lay in ambush in familial relationships and in the end assailed even the city with its deadly outcomes. "War at home," un-political in and of itself, thus became a political event.

It is precisely for this reason that Agamben refused to regard civil war as a simple family secret. He saw it instead as the threshold between the family and the state. When discord is unleashed, brothers kill each other as if they were enemies. Civil war makes it impossible to distinguish between inside and outside, home and state, the familiar and the foreign, blood relationships and citizenship. As political relationships forcefully invade the home, the family bond becomes even more estranged than the bond that separates warring political factions. Thus *stasis* is not war within the family; rather it is a device that functions "in a similar way to the state of exception."[12] This is how Agamben safeguards the irregularity of *stasis*.

The global civil war is the extension of *stasis* to the entire planet, by means of the incessant violence that pervades it, as if an epoch of absolute hostility had begun—so much so that one might think of the state of nature described by Hobbes in his *Leviathan*; except that that was a natural, pre-political violence that could be overcome by reason, while the current global violence follows upon political agreements—it is later, postmodern. This is because it is from modernity that the abyss upon which the political order of the world has been artificially constructed came to light. Hobbes offered another important suggestion in his *De cive* (2, 7, 11). Once a people is united under a sovereign, or in a democratic assembly, it becomes a multitude but is no longer a disunited multitude that precedes political agreement; it is a "dissolved multitude." Here one gets a glimpse of the threat of civil war, which always remains possible as long as the dissolved multitude inhabits the city-state.

The black banner of terror indicates the darkest and most brutal form of global civil war; it is its inexorable shadow, inscribed within its grammar, embedded in its logic. It lies hidden beneath outbursts of hostilities, it is aligned with the spurts of rage that stir up the stormy sea. The more politics assumes familial aspects and the world appears to be nothing but global management of the economy, the more terrorism becomes extreme, escalates, and erupts in its full, deadly potential.

# 4   The bomb of modernity

When we speak of modernity, we imagine a train that picks up speed after stopping at each station. It takes on the passengers who are waiting for it, exultant and festive as they stand on the platform. Some get into first-class cabins, others into second, others perhaps into third. But the train brings them all the light of reason and the equality of speed. It pulls them from old prejudices, cuts them away from habits and customs inherited from the past, emancipates them from the weight of tradition, liberates them from the yoke of religion. Once they have boarded the train, they are finally autonomous subjects who have stepped out of the age-old state of minority and are capable of evaluating critically everything that concerns them. They are ready to begin their life. No more impositions, no more chains, no more coercions. The passengers say farewell to the past, with no regrets. Full of hopeful expectations, they entrust themselves to the over-powering clatter of the train as it hurtles assuredly toward progress. Nothing can stop it, nothing can derail it. Expert machinists and able technicians are constantly improving the machinery, occasionally replacing the worn-out wheels with increasingly sophisticated, perfected equipment. Further checks are no longer required. The train of modernity speeds boldly toward final victory, nurturing faith in science, the certainty of improvements brought about by technology. The train's forward movement is a confirmation of pro-gress. Everyone on board is "progressive." How could it be otherwise? Freed from the fears that in the distant past were inculcated by religion, these passengers are no longer enslaved by arcane fears—so much so that, even as they savor the thrill of high velocity, they can nevertheless fall asleep, lulled by the ideology of comfort and by the safety of the "happy ending."

It is possible that they wake up only moments before the train suddenly explodes, like a projectile out of control, first rearing up and then twisting back on itself, almost as if it were taking a final glance at all that long road it has traveled before it is blown to smithereens. The progressivists' imagina-tion could never, even remotely, have foreseen such a tragic, inglorious end to this powerful convoy.

For the adepts of modernity, which is at once a conception of the world and above all a vision of history in which each epoch recapitulates and surpasses the preceding one, nothing could ever compromise the program of emancipation that had arisen from the Enlightenment. From this perspective, wars, massacres, and mass exterminations appear to be inci-dents along the way, irrational remnants of premodern bar-barity, pathological phenomena, moments of insanity that have not yet been vanquished—which is tantamount to expunging them from history and from reason. All this was considered to have happened in a time and place untouched by modernity. For a long while, it made possible a sanitized, reassuring image of human progress. But this image had already begun to disintegrate in the last century, during the two world wars, and especially after Auschwitz.

At that point philosophers began to divide into those who maintained intact their faith in the light of reason, treating extermination as a result of "madness" or "barbarism," and those who had already discerned in barbarism—and for some time—the hidden face, the dialectical other side of civilization; especially Walter Benjamin. And, following in his wake, beacons of fire—from Hannah Arendt to Günther Anders, from Theodor W. Adorno to Max Horkheimer and Herbert Marcuse—saw Auschwitz as an "administrative extermination" produced by modern western society in its most advanced stage.[13] In the gas chambers, the process of industrializing death, which during Hitler's regime functioned like an assembly line, took on the almost ritual precision of technology. These philosophers were the first to put modernity under indictment. For them, Auschwitz was not an aberration on the path of progress; on the contrary, it had sprung from instrumental reason. Therefore it could even constitute the kaleidoscope in which modernity could be observed. They recognized the traces of that self-destruction of reason that were increasingly evident after Hiroshima; they warned against the danger of getting blinded, caught in the illusion of those who mistakenly believed that they had defused the bomb of modernity.

Since that time, through ups and downs, the discussion around modernity has never stopped. The heated debate about "modern and postmodern," which was ignited in the 1980s by Jean-François Lyotard, proved to be only a new chapter.[14] Into the fray jumped Jürgen Habermas, who distanced himself from the Frankfurt School, although he had come from it, and defended modernity, considering it to be a still incomplete project. He harshly criticized the postmodernists—those "young conservatives" who, like Jacques Derrida and Michel Foucault, believed that the modern project had reached an end and, along with Nietzsche and Heidegger, denounced the self-destructive nature of modernity.[15]

This schism in philosophy has never really healed. Indeed, in some ways, it has grown and deepened. And it reemerged vividly when philosophers had to face the challenge of September 11, 2001.

## 5   The ghost of bin Laden

Ground Zero was covered by an immense mountain of smoking debris. The ruins of the World Trade Center burned for more than a hundred days. A bitter stench and a white powder—a mixture of concrete, asbestos, lead, fiberglass, cotton, kerosene, and the remains of the 2,749 human beings who had been pulverized in the towers—clogged the skies over Manhattan. Many of the bodies were never found. Each person who died had a particular story, each one reflected in his or her own way the complex multiplicity of a world that was becoming one—the Japanese sales clerk, the Ecuadorian chef, the Palestinian accountant, the Catholic chaplain, the stockbroker, the gay rights activist. Together they made up a small parliament. They represented 62 countries and almost all of the ethnic groups and religions of the world. The variety of their lives was living proof of a saying from the Quran [5:32] (and an earlier one from the Bible), according to which whoever kills an innocent person, it is as if he had killed all of humankind.

Al-Qaeda had wanted to topple the Twin Towers, a double image of the Tower of Babel. They had targeted America in that symbolic place, the center of the capital of the world, but in the end they struck all of humanity. "There is America, full of fear from its North to its South, from its West to its East. Thank God for that." Thus exulted Osama bin Laden, in a pre-recorded video broadcast by Al-Jazeera on October 7, 2001, the day after the first attacks unleashed by American and British bombers in Afghanistan. He then issued an appeal so that the event that had divided the world into believers and infidels would not be ignored. Along with his lieutenant Ayman al-Zawahiri, bin Laden waited in the caves of Tora Bora for the Mujahideen to rise up from one end of the earth to the other. It was in vain. He felt betrayed by the Muslims who had not hastened to join the ranks of his organization. Even the Taliban had abandoned him. The military defeat of al-Qaeda was crushing. But the Americans and their allies did not win either; they had not succeeded in capturing their prey. Bin Laden fled to Pakistan along with the last of the al-Qaeda combatants. It was on that occasion that he drew up a will in which, asking for his sons' forgiveness for his failure to devote more time to them and defending his choice to follow the call of jihad, he asserted that, in spite of those early painful reversals, a new era had begun that would lead to the downfall of the West within a few decades.

The "sheik of terror" was captured and killed on May 2, 2011 in Abbotabad, Pakistan, during an operation that had been planned for a long time by American intelligence and carried out by Navy Sea, Air, and Land Teams (SEALs) with the authorization of US President Barack Obama.

Today that event, which had to some degree been expected, seems almost like a déjà vu, a scene from a Hollywood catastrophe film. The ghost of Bin Laden continues to disturb the West, not so much on account of the form of terrorism that he inaugurated as for the victory that, as must be admitted by now, he achieved—a victory above all in the media. Broadcast live, the images of the two suicidal airplanes crashing into the Twin Towers, causing them to implode in a second suicide, appeared thousands of times on all the television screens in the world, in an infinite repetition never to be forgotten. This media victory, in all of its planetary dimensions and apocalyptic power, marked a historical victory because of its long-lasting traumatic effect.

# 6   Philosophies of terrorism

In the aftermath of the September 11 attacks, there unfolded an intense philosophical debate whose protagonists were Jürgen Habermas and Jacques Derrida. There emerged new reflections, which could only be called "philosophies of terrorism." This does not mean that in the past philosophy had not frequently dealt with the complex theme of terrorism. But the collapse of the Twin Towers, by calling modernity into question, had a direct impact on philosophy.

How can one judge that event, measure its effect, interpret its symbolic value and its political impact? These are the questions that oriented the interviews with Habermas and Derrida conducted by Giovanna Borradori and published in a book entitled *Philosophy in a Time of Terror*. It is worth noting that those who spoke out during the first few months after the September 11 attacks were two Europeans who were among the most prestigious exponents of continental philosophy at that time. The understandable caution detectable in their words also derived from a certain "foreignness" that they both acknowledged—an "outsider status," as Robert Esposito would say—which in this case was constituted by the Old World.[16] The America that had come under attack was being considered from the perspective of Europe and of European philosophy. If Derrida seemed more radical and clear in his political positions, it was nevertheless Habermas who pointed an accusatory finger at a certain form of patriotism of American intellectuals—and not only those who, like John Rawls and Michael Walzer, supported "just wars." In a critical tone, Habermas observed that "even leftist liberals for the moment seem to be in agreement with Bush's politics."[17]

Habermas has left open the question as to whether September 11, 2001 marked a turning point in history. While the September 11 attacks represented the "first event in world history" to take place on live television around the world, they should be seen, Habermas believes, in the context of the era of total war that had begun in 1914 and continued with totalitarian oppression, mechanized barbarity, and bureaucratic mass murder. For Habermas, the novelty of September 11 resided on the one hand in the symbolic power of the attacks, let alone of the targets that were struck, and on the other in the unprecedented profile of "global terrorism," which, not having a precise aim, cannot be defeated per se— unlike paramilitary actions linked to a national cause such as those of the Palestinians or the Chechens. This does not mean that al-Qaeda does not have political motivations—a fact that distinguishes terrorism from organized crime, for that matter (although at times the distinction between the two can be fluid). Preoccupied by the rule of law and by the risks of a "militant democracy," which by means of a perverse short-circuit denies democratic freedoms to the "enemies of democracy," Habermas sees unjust capitalistic modernization as the cause of Islamic fundamentalism and global terrorism. In his view, both are antimodern reactions to a perhaps too rapid process of inclusion, forms of "cognitive dissonance," in

other words temporary disturbances, pathologies that could
be overcome in the not yet completed progress of modernity.

It is precisely their way of seeing the relationship between
terror and modernity that separates the two philosophers. If
Habermas upholds a neo-Enlightenment conception, and
therefore regards globalization with a critical eye but with
unbroken trust, Derrida instead suspected that it is modern
rationality that contains the virus of terror within itself. In
this view, the perspective is turned upside down: it is not
modernity that can cure the pathology of terror, but rather
terror that is the symptom of modern pathology.

In highlighting the rhetoric of the American media, which
often use the formula "major event," Derrida emphasized the
risk of a merely quantitative valuation, recalling that "one
does not count the dead in the same way from one corner of
the globe to the other."[18] And he took up a word that had
been used by Heidegger: *Ereignis*, event. He saw September
11, 2001 as an unforeseeable "event" that interrupted and
shattered history. It is impossible to suppose that it can be
grasped, or fully understood; but on the other hand that
unforeseen interruption of history needs to be understood.
In a marginal note that has not lost its relevance, Derrida
stated that the ones to be called "philosophers" in the future
should be all those who know not only how to reflect in a
responsible way on the political issues of war and terrorism
but also how to keep firm —and indeed deepen—the distinction between understanding and justifying. One can and one
should try to understand, but this does not mean to justify.
Moral, or rather moralistic, condemnation has little to do
with philosophy.

A delayed result of the Cold War (when the United States
supported and provided arms to enemies of the Soviet Union),
the destruction of the Twin Towers represents two acts of
suicide in one: the suicide of the hijackers and the suicide
of those who trained them. Both committed acts of self-
destruction—as when a living organism eliminates the protection that should immunize it. Terrorism appears to be
the symptom of an autoimmune pathology whose carrier
is modernity.[19] A cure has not been discovered. But it is
certain that the consequences can be devastating, and not
only for democracy—because terror is the manifestation of

a resistance to modernization, severe to the point of putting the very existence of the world in jeopardy for the first time.

Situated far away from Habermas' view, Derrida's converges on many points with the interpretation of the French theorists of postmodernism, in particular with the vision of terrorism that Jean Baudrillard has been articulating for some time.

The Bataclan terrorists took the place of the musicians and occupied the stage, performing their own macabre drama. One thinks of Baudrillard's statement made years before: "The spectacle of terrorism forces the terrorism of spectacle upon us."[20] Unfortunately these words are all too often misunderstood, as if Baudrillard wanted to reduce terrorism to a spectacle, when in reality his intention was to denounce the obscenity of terrorism, which puts an end to any play and any illusion, yet through which terrorism exerts a certain moral fascination.

After the attack on the Twin Towers, Baudrillard was the first to come forth; and he offered a detailed diagnosis in his long article "L'Esprit du terrorisme," published in *Le Monde* on November 2, 2001. He unhesitatingly evaluated the impact of that event, contextualizing it within the theater of globalization. This is not surprising. Baudrillard was an explorer of "fatal strategies," an observer of "extreme phenomena"— anomalies, exceptions, incoherences, catastrophes, liminal cases, opaque and paroxystic events that upset the physical and metaphysical balance of the system. He was one of the few philosophers who had already written about terrorism.

Symbolic violence produced by hypermodernity, an explosive event that fits fully into the void of history, the convulsed face of low-level global war: terrorism was a "mirror" of evil for Baudrillard.[21] And he believed that it was a mistake to take one's eyes off of it. Intelligence about evil was for him a political imperative. The more the modern world stubbornly tries to make sure of everything that embodies the hyperbolic positivity of the good, from democracy to the free market, from human rights to individual liberty, by exorcising negative elements, the more the evil surfaces in all its terrifying virulence.

Baudrillard, a harsh critic of modernity, did not see the universe as dialectical but rather as tending toward extremes, consigned to a radical antagonism. Thus it did not make sense to him to seek syntheses and reconciliations. On the surface of a planet that is in the process of becoming one world, Baudrillard detected with far-seeing eyes the cracks that were opening, the schisms to come, the fault lines under the oceans. The Cold War was replaced by "pure war," as Paul Virilio has called it—that is, the hyperreal war that, by definition, will never be realized.[22] Thanks to mechanisms of mass destruction, there is no longer a place for *the* war, which can loom only in its dissuasive form. It will not be possible to circumscribe the wars that will break out in the future—they will not have an orbital dimension.

Beyond this point, in the history of the world, each event seems to be "without qualities," to use Robert Musil's expression: an event in itself, devoid of consequences. Nothing, for that matter, can ever effectively happen any more—the threat of a nuclear apocalypse is there to prevent it. Suspense becomes the timbre of existence. In spite of checks and preventative measures, the virtuality of catastrophe emerges everywhere. Security measures themselves might cause a disaster. Ours is the age of simulated catastrophes: the towering inferno that could annihilate New York, the earthquake that could tear Los Angeles apart. The virtual announces the real. The cancellation of the negative, the concealment of crisis—these open the vortex of catastrophe. The tremors on the surface are the signs of a disequilibrium, of a spasmodic motion—territories that smash into one another, tectonic plates that slide over one another, erratic ice packs—as the globalized universe seems to plunge into the void.

In this context of fluctuating capitals, uninterrupted information, and dominance of technology, terror erupts as an inexplicable anomaly, almost as if it were a phenomenon that had come from somewhere else.

# 7   Red Brigades, the Red Army Faction (RAF), and the impossible exchange

As early as the 1970s, Baudrillard was shedding light on the secret workings of terrorism. During the so-called "red decade," there was no shortage of cases upon which to reflect;

but it was the kidnapping of Aldo Moro in Italy on March 16, 1978 that led Baudrillard to consider the figure and the decisive role of the hostage.

In a world in which everything can be exchanged, the hostage breaks the chain, making exchange impossible. Certainly the tactic is not original; in the past, too, hostages were captured and then used to negotiate exchanges. But the Moro case was completely unprecedented precisely because negotiation was impossible; in fact it was radically refused. Thus the hostage taking was purely symbolic. Calculations and exchanges were ignored. The system—bypassed, circumvented, sidestepped—entered into a paralyzing impasse; it was incapable of responding. The challenge, unforeseeable and deadly, did not admit a response—unless the system were ready to let itself implode.

"This was the triumph of the Red Brigades," wrote Baudrillard.[23] As soon as Aldo Moro was kidnapped, he was already out of play. He represented the empty state, the null equivalent of a power that had been annulled in its sovereignty because it had been taken hostage. How, by whom, and for whom could Moro have been exchanged? The symbolic challenge of the Red Brigades, which annulled every rule, was an "attack on the heart of the state," but one performed on a revolving stage where power and counterpower alternated in obsolete, passé roles, both revealing themselves to be impotent, incapable of exchanging anything. The hostage, with whom nothing could be done, became an encumbrance. If Moro had been released, the state might even have feared contamination. His body was obscenely abandoned in the trunk of a car: a defeat for the Red Brigades, the illusion of a terrorism that could no longer turn the hostage to any real advantage.

Hence the difficulty of freeing hostages—for example those taken by the guerrilla group FARC (Fuerzas Armadas Revolucionarias de Colombia), such as Ingrid Betancourt, kidnapped and kept in isolation for more than six years, from 2002 to 2008. A hostage is a sort of talisman, an almost "sacred" fetish, so precious as to have no price, impossible to possess or exchange, and therefore no less dangerous and irreducible than a terrorist. The hostage is the alter ego of the terrorist; the terrorist is the alter ego of the hostage.[24] A unique complicity unites them. Their lives, bound together by an unbreakable thread, are dedicated to the same sacrificial epilogue. From time to time, the state will choose to suppress one or the other.

The terrorist and the hostage represent an exception to the rule of exchange; they belong to a zone where it is impossible to trade. They reveal the deception of reciprocity, the illusion of a subject who, albeit alienated, could still negotiate from the heights of its autonomy and sovereignty. They point an accusatory finger at the chimera, long gone, of the social contract; they unmask its liberal nostalgia. They trigger speculation in all its senselessness, unveiling a radical state of emergency.

The Red Brigades inaugurated the age of postmodern terror. For the first time, real political order was challenged by a symbolic act. And just as exchange was impossible, so was meeting the challenge. If the Italian state, stripped naked in its impotence, had reacted, it would have accelerated the spiral of empowerment; it would have become terror to the second power, more terrorist than the terrorists themselves. This is why every ultimatum is never really the last and must be disregarded. All the violence mobilized by the Italian state—police, army, institutions—could do nothing against that single symbolic act. Although the relationship of power was totally asymmetrical, the state apparatus was in danger of collapsing. The challenge—symbolic, yet effectively deadly—dragged the Italian government to a place where to respond would have meant to destroy itself. It was checkmate for the state.

But it was also checkmate for the Red Brigades. Their desperate attempt to radicalize the clash ended in nothing. The Red Brigades' mistake was to believe that they could really put an end to the system. But the revolution gave way to symbolic subversion—in the end, that utopian act, that dream of an exchange, was proof of the impossibility of an exchange. As deflagrating as it was, like the blast of an explosion, the symbolic act was, ultimately, an event without consequences. It was part of a fatal strategy, irresistible and pernicious, ineluctable and deadly. The symbolic act carried its own end and was oriented by the end, or rather by the ending: the death that underlay it.

The terrorist is ready to die. This is his extreme challenge: a gift that goes beyond the economy of exchange and to which the state cannot respond, except with an equal or greater death. In short, when faced with the challenge of terrorism, the state is called upon to commit suicide. The response of the state, which arms itself with the same terror, would be its own death and its own collapse.

Baudrillard analyzed the German Federal Republic and the actions carried out, in a crescendo, by the Red Army Faction (RAF), also known as the Baader–Meinhof Group. It was 1977. The fatal strategy of the RAF had already produced a series of impossible negotiations; hostages were taken in order to demand the release of RAF members from the maximum security prison at Stammheim. On September 5, the RAF kidnapped Hanns Martin Schleyer, a former SS officer, president of the Confederation of German Employers' Associations (Bundesvereinigung der Deutschen Arbeitgeberverbände, BDA) and of the Federation of German Industries (Bundesverband der Deutschen Industrie, BDI). Schleyer's body would be found 43 days later, when he no longer served any purpose as a hostage. On October 13 of that same year, a Lufthansa airplane [*sc.* traveling from Palma de Mallorca to Frankfurt] was highjacked and flown to Mogadishu Airport. In exchange for the passengers, the Palestinian highjackers demanded the release of the militants from the Baader–Meinhof Group. But all negotiations came to nothing. The events condensed into a single date: October 18, 1977. That night, German special forces in Mogadishu liberated the hostages and killed three of the four terrorists who had highjacked the plane. During those same hours, in the Stammheim prison, RAF leaders Andreas Baader, Gudrun Ensslin, Jan-Carl Raspe, and Imgard Möller learned the outcome of the blitz, according to the official version. The next morning, Baader and Ensslin were found dead in their cells. Raspe was found in his death throes, and died shortly afterward. Möller was taken to the hospital with four knife wounds in her chest, and survived. This was the "suicide night" with which the German Autumn came to an end. But was it really suicide?

LAWYER 1: A German autumn. The utopia of the revolution of 1968 was buried with the funeral of Andreas, Gudrun, and Jan. The utopia of a generation that had dreamed of a completely new society.

WIEGAND: The sinister shadow of Stalin has put on a parka and concealed his face behind a Palestinian keffiyeh. To live his own passion for justice all the way, to the extreme. OK. But the Utopia of '68 was compromised the moment that rage turned into terrorism. I prefer to echo Rosa Luxemburg, who said that "freedom is always and exclusively freedom for the one who thinks differently."

LAWYER 2: Irmgard Möller survived. Jan-Carl Raspe was still alive, but he died in the hospital. To the best of my knowledge, Baader, in cell number 719, had succeeded in concealing a 7.65 FÉG pistol in his record player. To simulate a gun battle, he first fired into his mattress, then into the wall next to the window. He picked up the bullet casings and placed them next to himself. Then he re-loaded the gun, sat down on the floor, pointed the barrel at the nape of his neck and pulled the trigger. [...]

LAWYER 1: Andreas Baader, Gudrun Ensslin, and Jan-Carl Raspe were murdered by the servants of the capitalist state, by those bastards, the police and the judges, and their murder was made to look like suicide.

LAWYER 2: Collective suicide signifies resistance unto death. The body is the ultimate weapon against the oppression of the capitalist state. Like during hunger strikes. A revolutionary never gives up. This makes him invincible.[25]

The act of repression followed the act of terrorism in vain. Nor did it matter, according to Baudrillard, how the "facts" had occurred. Whether or not Andreas Baader had been "liquidated" was a question to be left for the "vultures of the truth,"[26] because it would mean reducing to the political order of power the symbolic challenge that deflagrates in all of its implosive virulence: the death of the terrorist. The violence of the state risks being sucked back into the symbolic challenge. Baader's purported suicide, possibly enacted by the German state, which in turn simulated the fatal strategy of terror, played a decisive role: this unresolved death started a vertiginous cycle with no return.

# 8   The absolute weapon of one's own death

What could the terrorism of the late twentieth century have in common with the terrorism of the new millennium? After

September 11, 2001, Ground Zero, the name that had once been given to the land and sea epicenter of a future atomic explosion, denoted the place in which the two towers of the world's greatest superpower had been blown to smithereens. Ground Zero is the symbolic vertex of the collapse of an epoch, the point zero touched by the black light of terror.

Baudrillard evaluated that "event" without reducing it to a pathology of reason, but also without making of it a unicum in the history of human destruction. After a long period when "events were on strike," to use the powerful expression of the Argentine philosopher Macedonio Fernández, after a period of collective wishing that nothing more would happen and yet that, much to the contrary, the always-the-same would be interrupted by a definitive structure, the event that had been presaged, imagined, even dreamed of occurred, in an unconfessable complicity with the terrorist strategy, which contributed to explaining its huge resonance in the media.

Continuities and differences should not be overlooked. For Baudrillard, contemporary terrorism was "contemporaneous with globalization."[27] So it becomes necessary to ask how that extreme phenomenon has been modified by the unification of the world. And yet the theoretical matrix is the same as the one with which Baudrillard interpreted the terrorism of the Red Brigades and of the RAF. In both cases, the ruling political order was held in check through a symbolic challenge to which it was impossible to respond. Thus the new global terrorism follows in the wake of twentieth-century terrorism. The difference is not radical; rather we are dealing here with the further radicalization of a challenge already launched, albeit in other contexts, with different meanings and goals. But the novelty is limited and the fatal strategy is in fact the same, just as the vertiginous cycle that it sets in motion is the same. The generalized system of exchange is suddenly stopped by the unexpected gesture of the terrorist who offers up his own death—a sacrifice impossible to reciprocate. Indeed, it would be like asking the system to commit suicide, when suicide—one's own self-destruction—is the only forbidden thing, the only recondite prohibition.

In a hyperbolic rebooting that is part and parcel of the apparatus of terrorism, suicide is no longer "pure loss." The terrorist turns his own death into the absolute weapon of an offensive that is without precedent, both in its form and in its efficacy. To kill oneself in order to kill—that is the radicalization.

The system had almost reached perfection and was therefore vulnerable everywhere, given that even the tiniest spark could ignite a cosmic deflagration. The system reacted to this unprecedented situation by becoming rigid, terrorized in its own turn; it contracted, it contorted itself in its own violence, experiencing its own inability to react, letting itself be tempted by its own useless hyperefficiency. Baudrillard employed the metaphor of tetanus: he spoke of a power that was prey to compulsive spasms, infected by the wound in its depths, at the mercy of the contractions of tetanus, infected by the toxin against which it launched all its antibodies. Baudrillard saw terrorism as a virus that causes a spastic paralysis of power. It is not only a symbolic act, nor merely a challenge impossible to meet: it is an immune or autoimmune reaction. In this last mode of considering the extreme phenomenon of terror, Baudrillard's philosophical judgment converged to a great extent with that of Derrida.

The symbolic challenge, which already in the recent past could not be met, has now reached a further, unprecedented potential through globalization, where terror is no longer seen as an unusual event on the path to irreversible progress. Evil, which it was believed could be definitively defeated in the glow of global order, rises up irrevocably; it shows its most chilling face, with the dark, grim countenance of the damned, promising this time to have a perpetual, pervasive presence. It is terror that proclaims its "no" to violent globalization, putting the whole world at risk for the first time.

# 9   Atmoterrorism: Auschwitz, Dresden, Hiroshima, and so on

Is there a connection between technology and terrorism? What kind of impact could the dazzling successes of technology have had on the concept of terror, as they gave rise to a new praxis of extermination?

To give a reply, it would be necessary to review the evolution of weapons, the mechanisms of war, beginning with bombs and poison gas. This is what Peter Sloterdijk has done, reflecting upon the manipulation of the air that has forever put an end to the ingenuous privilege once enjoyed by human beings before the caesura of the twentieth century: the privilege of breathing without having to worry about what might be in the surrounding atmosphere.

Sloterdijk has no doubts: terrorism is the "child of modernity."[28] But this filial relationship emerged in an explicit way only in the twentieth century. This is why purely modern terror is a post-Hegelian phenomenon, which therefore cannot be placed in immediate continuity with the Reign of Terror under the Jacobins in 1793 France, or with the Bolshevik revolution of 1917. Nor should it be confused with the "order of terror"—to use a well-known definition formulated by Wolfgang Sofsky—that was constructed by Hitler's dictatorship.[29]

What distinguishes terror in the age of technology from all its precursors is the assault on the environment. For the first time, it is not the enemy that is targeted—it is the atmosphere, the very air that the enemy breathes. In this sense, it would be legitimate to speak of "atmoterrorism." When did this new modality of extermination begin? Is it possible to pinpoint a date? Sloterdijk situates the "primal scene" during World War I. It took place in Ypres, on the western front, in the course of the battle of April 22, 1915, between 6:00 and 7:00 p.m. A favorable wind blowing from the German lines toward the Allied trenches pushed clouds of chlorine gas that had been released from more than 5,700 cylinders. The hands of the clock marked a profound caesura: the beginning of technical extermination. From that moment on, the praxis of terror—brought as a dowry by the history of civilization—was to embody the originality of the twentieth century better than any other phenomenon.

Sloterdijk meticulously reproduces that first large-scale use of chemical weapons. The notion of a duel, which for some time had still offered the image of a manly, honest clash between two opponents, was abandoned as the interaction between enemies evolved on a post-military basis. The trigger was the fact that the soldiers on either side were unreachable to those on the other side: they remained hidden behind the trenches for months. No long-range weapons in use at that time would have been sufficient; modern chemical warfare, a precursor to aerial bombardment, provided the solution. The use of poison gas, increasingly widespread in spite of Article 23A of the Laws and Customs of War on Land of the Hague Convention, acted in turn as an incentive to the study of toxic clouds and to the theory of unbreathable spaces.

When considered from this perspective, modern terrorism reveals itself to be another, more powerful form of warfare. From a circumscribed violence of war is unleashed the freedom to exterminate: absolute annihilation, unbound by any impediments, physical or metaphysical. The transition is completed when leave is definitively taken of the contest between adversaries, of the encounter between regular troops. Free from any rules, terror rages. But modern terror, in which the knowledge of extermination is condensed while the age-old character of the attack is still preserved, has an unprecedented novelty. The enemy's body is not necessarily liquidated by direct blows. Rather the environment in which the enemy lives is attacked; his or her existence is rendered impossible. The assault upon the body's vital functions, from respiration to the central nervous system, makes it appear that the enemy is falling under his or her own impulse—for example, the natural impulse to breathe. Responsibility is shattered; it becomes anonymous. And the asymmetry of the opposing forces becomes increasingly irrelevant. In fact it takes only one terrorist to carry out an attack of devastating effects. This should not, however, lead us to believe that terror is the weapon of the weak. Historically, it has been nations that have made ample use of terrorist methods throughout the twentieth century.

When technology with all its destructive potential bursts forth and shatters the framework of war, violence multiplies; it becomes violence against people, against things—indiscriminate violence that envelops all of life. The exercise of terror, which is always conceived of as a counterattack and never as a gratuitous initial assault, is the willingness to enlarge the zone of combat—without limits. Here the enemy is not even an "enemy" any longer, so trenches and front lines have no meaning. The other becomes merely an entity to be eliminated. There is no question of taking this entity prisoner, defeating it, depriving it of its liberty. Rather—and what is much more—it is a matter of liberating the environment— even the planet—of the other and of this person's liberty. This epochal change enshrines the transition from traditional warfare to the kind of warfare that, unchained and rendered explicit by technology, becomes exterminism: a program of annihilation.

Into the history of technical exterminism, which reached an extreme example on September 11, 2001 and has persisted into the twenty-first century, Sloterdijk inserts episodes that are apparently distant from one another and not always viewed contiguously, from the yellowish–white cloud of gas that assailed the French and Canadian troops on the other side of the trenches at Ypres to the industrialized use of Zyklon B—the notorious hydrogen cyanide, used at first (as promised by the companies that produced it) to make environments *mottenfrei* ("worm-free") and, later, to make the entire planet *judenfrei* ("Jew-free"), according to the dictates of the Final Solution.

Sloterdijk highlights other memorable dates from that span of time—for example, February 8, 1924, when the state of Nevada began operating the first gas chamber for civil executions, introducing atmoterrorism into the penal code of a democracy. That model was followed by other states, including California. The electric chair—a euphemism for the powerful charges of electricity that fry the brain of a condemned prisoner—was replaced by the more ascetic gas chamber, in which the exhalations of gas block the transport of oxygen to the blood so that the prisoner dies of internal asphyxiation. The new method was seen as having a certain "humanism"— a sentimental law of progressive modernity.

Technical atmoterrorism made the administering of the death penalty by gas more neutral and impersonal, facilitating the transition to a veritable mass production of cadavers in Hitler's death camps. There are reliable statistics from Auschwitz-Birkenau documenting the fact that, in a single night in 1943, from the 13th to the 14th of April, 1,492 Jews from the ghetto in Cracow were gassed with six kilos of Zyklon B. The assembly line then delivered the remains to be incinerated in Crematorium II.

Sloterdijk is one of those philosophers who, in the wake of Heidegger, followed the thread of technology and dared to write the names of other places alongside Auschwitz: Dresden, Hiroshima, Nagasaki. These cities were the stages of a grim meteorology of aerial bombardments that, doing away with spatial distance, struck previously inaccessible places and shattered the distinction between civilians and combatants. The globalization of war was achieved only through long-range aerial weapons. This time terror was no longer an attack on the air conducted from the ground; it was an attack from the air that would have as its target an entire way of life, declared inimical and therefore eliminated. From a philosophical point of view, then, aeronautics played a decisive role. After describing the destruction of Guernica on April 26, 1937 by the Condor Legion, a Nazi aviation unit, Sloterdijk reconstructs the bombing of Dresden on the night of February 13/14, 1945.

The airplanes of the Royal Air Force had a rigorously conceived plan: to surround the city of Dresden with a ring of incendiary bombs capable of producing a firestorm unleashed from above that would have the effect of an enormous blast furnace. More than 650,000 bombs were dropped in the first two attacks. The intention to strike the civilian population was clear, all the more as it was known that thousands of refugees were massed in the area around the central station. According to the most conservative estimates, there were at least 35,000 victims. Many were burned to death, their bodies charred; others, who had not come into contact with the flames, were found dead of dehydration, or mummified. Because of the heat, the air-raid shelters were transformed into ovens where more than 10,000 people roasted to death or were asphyxiated by toxic fumes. The entire city center was like a combustion chamber. But Dresden was not an exception or a parodistic anomaly; rather it provided a new model of thermo-terrorism. Nations had begun to use terrorist methods, and Sloterdijk does not hesitate to define Churchill as a "terrorist." For that matter, the British prime minister himself would not have hesitated to admit it.[30]

Looked at in this exegetic line, the dropping of atomic bombs on Hiroshima and Nagasaki carried out by the Americans on August 6 and 9, 1945, which is usually considered an unparalleled, one-of-a-kind event, appears instead as a qualitative rather than a quantitative escalation. It is estimated that there were approximately 100,000 victims at Hiroshima and 40,000 at Nagasaki. But the numbers skyrocket when those who subsequently died of radioactive contamination are taken into account. This was the first nuclear attack against an entire way of life, the provisory culmination of modern exterminism. Radioactive weapons and the aftereffects of their use represented the novelty. The bombings of Hiroshima and Nagasaki were followed by a black rain that fell inexorably on the devastated area, bringing with it previously unknown illnesses, deep ulcerations, cancerous tumors, and unexplained burns, as if a hidden enemy had continued to strike in an imperceptible atmosphere of waves and rays.

## 10   Heidegger and the ban of existence from the biosphere

Radiation terrorism has left a legacy consisting of its own aftereffects—an invisible aggression, an attack on the most infinitesimal level, with immeasurable effects. Whether state-sponsored or not, the most recent terrorism has brought about increases in the ability to assail the biosphere. What is more, unbeknownst to public opinion worldwide, the American superpower has developed new strategies for a future ionospheric war—strategies capable of making military use of the climate, for example by modifying severe weather by blocking precipitation. Bioterrorism in its crudest form—the spreading of viruses and bacteria—is now flanked by more refined, secret forms, including sonic weapons that can act from a distance on human organs, particularly the brain—that is, neurotelepathic weapons.

What is important for existence is the fact that postmodern terror possesses the unmistakable peculiarity of targeting not only the enemy's body but also the environment in which the enemy lives. It goes without saying that, for this new form of global war, which leaves every other war behind, to win means to annihilate, even at the cost of self-annihilation. Existence is plunged into an unlivable environment in which it can collapse in an instant or succumb later as a result of lethal aftereffects. Immunization is worthless. The new weapons of terror philosophically seek out further vulnerable points in the conditions of life. Transforming the intimate places in which existence used to dwell almost ingenuously, the terrorist becomes the dark shadow of the philosopher.

Heidegger had used the term "countryside" to indicate the place where, in spite of the lack of a homeland that had become the destiny of the world in the age of technology, anyone could find refuge. For him, that refuge was a wooded clearing in a forest. But beyond this idyllic vision of his, which is often misunderstood, Heidegger is the only philosopher to have foreseen the threat that technology represents for human life. After the terrorist episodes of recent decades, we can detect in his "displacement" [*"spaesatezza"*] not the lost and unrecoverable sojourn in his rural cottage,[31] but rather the progressive banishment of existence from all the safety niches of the natural biosphere, with no possibility of finding a place that has been preserved or of reaching the source of some miraculous immunization.

While there is no doubt that there is a connection between technology and terror, the further step taken by Sloterdijk is more problematic. He sees in terrorism a modus operandi, a modality of acting—or, better, of proceeding.[32] Sloterdijk's legitimate intention is to warn against the common expression "war on terror," which makes no sense because it raises to the status of an enemy a method that is widely used by many parties. And yet, lurking in Sloterdijk's position is the risk of making terror into a strictly technical thing, of neutralizing it and reducing it to a mechanism that continues to operate almost independently of historical contexts and political agents by taking different forms, increasingly intense and extreme. This is the kind of attitude of indifference toward technology that can also be found in Heidegger; and it explains why Sloterdijk, in writing about the extermination carried out by the Nazis, maintains that "the Hitler factor" merely marks "an escalating element."[33] It also clarifies the dispassionate distance with which Sloterdijk seems to limit the significance of the attack on the Twin Towers and, more generally, his tendency to downplay Islamism, which he sees as incapable of becoming the "new World Bank of dissidence"[34]—almost as if the challenge of jihad could in essence be relegated to the status of a phenomenon that can be overcome in a short time and, in part, has already been surpassed.

## 11   The monopoly of negation

The "global age"—this is what some, starting with the British sociologist Martin Albrow, have called the current era. For others, it is the "second ecumene," the time of "post-history," that time after 1945 during which the Old World has exhausted its capacity to attack, having expended all of its energy in two world wars. Thus came to an end the expansionist aspirations that had begun in 1492 with the four voyages of Columbus. History coincided with the hybrid epos of conquest in all its victorious unilateralism, as it was dictated by its heroes; and it came to an end when planet Earth became the "world" for everyone. Globalization is a *fait accompli*; what is more, it is an irreversible axiom.

Having been circumnavigated and traveled from top to bottom, the world has become a system that is kept together by a tight network of traffic, connected through flows of communication, and permeated by the liquidity of capital. Post-history is the epoch in which globalization proclaims its inexorable progress, giving the lie to any alternative. The movements that criticize its dysfunctions do nothing more than certify that it functions. It is impossible to go back. Globalization has risen to the level of destiny for a humanity that is not only constrained to live in a synchronized world, where time is bent to a perpetual state of actuality, but also obliged to cohabit in a space of unknown density, where one is no longer immune from the other and from encounters with the other. Sociability and moral obligation give way to widespread misanthropy. The global village is no longer human, as McLuhan and other optimistic theorists of the media had predicted. A global community caught in a powerful logical synthesis, forced into a compulsory abstraction, assailed by insistent messages, devoid of universal validity has been produced instead. The planet no longer offers this community an intimate way of being at home, a reassuring being with oneself, because it has been reduced to an external place, a place of permanent exchange—a crowded, inhospitable global market square.

Triumphant march toward generalized comfort, improved quality of life, modernization, scientific advancement, new technological developments, extension of democracy, expansion of human rights, unstoppable progress of reason and its lights: globalization has affirmed itself as the great triumph of the good. In this world system not even a shadow of evil should have remained; all of it, to the tiniest particles, should have been eliminated, exterminated. A radiant, transparent, shining universe should have ratified the final defeat of evil.

This moralizing version of globalization, marked as it is by the common sense of an unshakeable modernism, sees only perfection in the future but believes, in true Manichaean spirit, that it can detect and defeat the dark forces that continue to resist. Faults, collapses, fractures, unexplained contrapositions, previously nonexistent borders, unthought-of obstacles—those who believe in the moralizing version of globalization close their eyes to all of this, in the name of a calculated management of progress at any cost. And yet the devastating effects of this supremacy of positiveness emerge violently and are transmitted by contagion. Prophylactic measures and cosmetic surgery on the negative have served no purpose.

In fact the opposite has happened. In the globalized world, upon which the imperative of continuous daylight has been forced and the diffusion of artificial light has been imposed, it never stopped being night in those parts that were already in shadow. And the sparks of evil that have accumulated in the heart of modern unhappiness, becoming more and more incandescent, have triggered a new combustion—because evil, as Dostoyevsky and Nietzsche knew, is not only a moral criterion but also a principle of imbalance, a source of vertigo that can also turn into a state of mind. In the post-historical age, the decision to disregard evil has contributed to evil's inexorable vengeance. Exorcized, tabooed, silenced, evil has burst forth again, with a surplus of energy, in the midst of a supposedly harmonious conviviality, taking unprecedented forms, eruptive and expansive, in an ecstatic crescendo.

Evil proclaims its "no" to the integration of world order that has been achieved: in acts of random destruction, in the negativity of the unemployed, in the malaise of all of its declinations—none of this coalesces in the form of protest. In fact the protest against globalization is part of globalization itself: anti-globalization movements can be considered an internal peripeteia that is repeatedly overcome. Paradoxically, this is the limit to the positive proposals of resistance, whose political impact is diminished when faced with the system, which remains master of the game.

Terrorism is the form taken by revenge against the monopoly of denial. It is revenge on behalf of all the forces that have been humiliated by the world system; it is a radical antagonism that emerges within the system itself, in the internal dissociation of a power that discovers itself to be powerless in its uncontrolled convulsion. Terror is heterogeneous, because it originates from an irreducible symbolic order; in its virulent refractoriness, it is the specter that keeps the world in a constant state of checkmate.

This means that, from its extraterritorial place, terror rules the order of the world. It makes the world into a hostage that is subject to perennial blackmail. It terrorizes the world, plunging it into an obsession with security and forcing it to surrender to a planetary police network. Is this the victory of terrorism? In the constellation of terror, it is no longer possible to speak of victory or defeat—only of empowerment. There is no response to terror except its own incessant intensification.

## 12   The metaphysics of the terrorist attack

The hyperbolic violence of terrorism, which is a form of political violence, should be scrutinized and studied in the context of globalization, where every fault line, every refractory zone, every ripple of the stormy sea can be a source of terror. From one moment to another, the specter of terrorism can rise up, be unleashed, explode. How can we see clearly amid smoke and miasma, amid obfuscation and devastation? And yet the secret of terrorism is contained on this stage, and it is there that it should be decrypted. The scene: an attempted terrorist attack.

Certainly, as Baudrillard suggested, the terrorist carries out a symbolic act. But, upon close consideration, a revolutionary act is also symbolic, and in the end revolution itself, insofar as it may open a new world, can be seen as a symbolic form of politics. Thus Baudrillard's definition is not sufficient. And yet it is undeniable that terrorism sustains the primacy of the act. Whether it tacitly presupposes the act or celebrates it as an encomium, a terrorist attempt is an act for its own sake, an injunction to pure action.

To deconstruct the purported supremacy of the terrorist act, to shed light on the violence that underlies it, it is indispensable—as Lenin already knew well—to place it in the framework of a political reading of history.[35] Only in this way does that act, which aspires to be pure, take on more precise contours—less abstract and above all less immaculate.

The terrorist takes one by surprise; as he or she moves into action, the terrorist gains an advantage. The act itself is already a weapon. Terrorist action has the character of an attempt. Its etymology makes this clear: the Latin noun *attentatum*, from the verb *attemptare*, means trial, attempt. After having observed the enemy's conditions of life, the terrorist attempts to exploit those conditions in order to strike unexpectedly, to carry out a treacherous ambush. The terrorist makes an attempt on the life of others—even at the price of sacrificing his or her own life.

The political question is about the meaning of that act, the goal of that attempt. Is the new fiction still timely, when the final bell of the "grand narratives" diagnosed by Lyotard has already tolled? Is there still room for a terrorist act in the asphyxiating space of globalization, where the earth has been occupied and divided up and the new order has been defined and imposed, although it often turns out to be a confused chaos?

Terrorism is condensed in an act that is first and foremost an attempt to find a single direction and a single meaning in the global scenario. It is an effort to simplify what is complicated, a way of putting a limit to the unlimited, of drawing front lines, of setting apart the enemy—in a way that is not all that different from what its declared enemies plan to do. It is a paradoxical attempt to divert the course of history forcibly, an anachronistic ambition to rewrite its last chapters. The metaphysics of the terrorist attack is the will to power that, by attacking, makes the decision to overcome the void of inertia. It is the revendication of offensive violence and of the irrecoverable advantage that is gained by those who get there first; it is the assymetrical euphoria of aggression.

It should be very clear that the political model for the metaphysics of the terrorist attack is not revolution—neither the one of 1798 nor the one of 1917. Rather it is the European expansion, which, from 1492 onward, crossing the tropics and the meridians, never stopped until globalization became a *fait accompli*. The reaction of the new agents of global terror has been to reproduce the original act of that expansion. In this way modern-day terrorism, even in its most radical form, is profoundly reactionary, both in its philosophical underpinnings and in its political schema.

But this counterexpansion inevitably appears to be belated and random, given that there is nothing left to divide and there is not one inch of earth that hasn't already been conquered and occupied—except for the information space that has opened up in the planetary universe, that boundless "McWorld" where global terror has been able to raise its threatening flag, more disquieting than the Black Standard of the self-styled territorialized Islamic state. The invasion of the infosphere, which is almost devoid of barriers and without defenses, is not an arduous undertaking. With minimal attacks and telegenic explosions, the terrorists of the new millennium can destabilize the entire system, taking the world hostage. They have on their side the media, which, unable to create all their stories in the studio, are supplied with events to report about by the impresarios of real violence. This explains the enormous success of the strategy of expansion followed by terrorism, even without necessarily boasting territorial conquests.

Success in the media, however, should not mislead us. The metaphysics of the terrorist attack remains—just as there remains faith in the attack, the will to strike first, the ideology of freedom of action. In this respect in particular, terrorism and neoliberalism are like the recto and verso of the same sheet of paper. Both are the most recent versions of a philosophy of action that is summed up in the intent to be like rays of free and pure initiative, subjects of sovereign aggressiveness. The basis of a terrorist attack, the impatient credo of making the first move, lead to mistaking the political void for an open field.

The terrorist challenge seems to emerge more clearly from the extinguished flames and foul fumes of the attack itself. A terrorist attack is not only a symbolic action; it also advances a presumption of sovereignty. It is an act that wants to be sovereign, *superanus* in the etymological sense—superior, supreme, and extreme. Historically speaking, it is carried out on the modern political scene in different forms and modalities whereby power displays the void upon which it is founded. It is not a revolutionary act, nor is it an act of insurrection. It has nothing to do with initiatory violence, except for the negation that it violently captures and magnetizes in that moment. The scenario in which the terrorist act takes place is that of a sovereign confrontation. The more the sovereignty that it challenges is delegitimized, destabilized, and wavering, the more does terrorism push to advance its claims. It is as if it were announcing the last state, as if it were revealing a state that has reached its limit; as if it were the observer and indicator of an evil sovereignty. This is what happens in the globalized world, where the established sovereignty, put into play by the push toward the unlimited, emptied and paralyzed, is confronted by the spectral power of Islamic terror. A terrorist attack is not even an explosion; upon close consideration, it is an implosive form within the political void. Far from anarchy, which reveals the abyss of sovereignty in order to turn it against the state, global terrorism seeks to appropriate that sovereignty—its origins, its command—and to take its place. It enters into competition with the powers that be by using their own weapons; it challenges them on their own territory. In the end, the one who is sovereign is the one who poses the most credible threat. Terrorism is the specter of modern sovereignty, which, in turn, is always potentially terrorist.

# 2

# Terror, Revolution, Sovereignty

Attacks almost always end up having an impact upon forces that are completely different from those originally targeted by the perpetrators. They influence not so much the course of history as its rhythm, sometimes accelerating it, sometimes slowing it down.

Ernst Jünger[1]

## 1   A brand name

"Terrorist attack on the Zaventem Airport in Brussels." "Terrorism alert in London." Images of devastation flash on the television screen. The announcer emphasizes: "New security measures have been taken." He reports that "police and army personnel will surveil the zones that are at risk."

Events like these follow closely one after the other. Not a day goes by when global violence does not manifest itself in its most extreme and unpredictable forms, in a crescendo that leaves us stunned, dismayed, almost inert. Fear takes over, disorientation prevails. Those gratuitous acts of cruelty, those scenes of war outside war zones, those atrocious crimes that break into everyday life—it all seems senseless, irrational, inexplicable. Television broadcasts and newspaper headlines speak about "terrorism," and the term abounds on social networks. Twitter and Facebook users click, share, comment, and automatically forward the official nomenclature: "terrorism."

There is no time left to reflect on the plausibility of the term, much less to consider possible alternatives. In fact there is no time to think at all. We unthinkingly use a keyword that promises to provide access to a range of phenomena, at times very different and perhaps even incomparable; we resort to using an ambiguous and indistinct word as a universal skeleton key, a passe-partout that designates and expresses all the anxieties of our age.

Whether it indicates intellectual laziness, political acquiescence, a need to make the unknown known, or an impasse of language, which is unable to keep up with a reality more and more atrociously fractured and disjointed, that term, *terrorism*, omnipresent and uncontested, dominates the public sphere; there is no doubt about it. Again and again we hear "terrorism," again and again "war on terrorism."

There seems to be nothing beyond this sort of closing credit that summarizes the "events of the day," to which the ontology of the present is reduced. It is the nothingness of terror that looms, horrible and paralyzing. What could there possibly be to understand, to interpret, to think? On the one hand, mangled corpses that elicit only pity; on the other, an enigma locked in a black box that the experts will open sooner or later, to shed light on what has happened. That is all. And that is enough for public opinion.

There certainly will not be any shortage of conspiracy theorists, as ever. In fact terrorism, precisely because it seems to elude any rational schema of cause and effect, feeds fantasies, fables, and conspiracy theories of every kind. The notion of a conspiracy—that magical vision of history in which everything can be related to a single cause that acts intentionally, with a persevering will—has never been as widespread as it has been since September 11, 2001. Who is behind all those inexperienced, bumbling terrorists? So bumbling, in fact, that Anis Amri left his identity card in the truck he used in the attack on the Christmas market in Berlin. The Internet swarms with jokes and satirical cartoons on this topic.

Were it not for the obscure, perverse, nihilistic destructiveness with which terrorism is always connected, it would not even be a philosophical theme. It would not merit reflection, but only blame. In the realm of philosophy perhaps more than elsewhere, thinking about terrorism is suspect. To try to understand is to get too close to the slippery slope of justification, with the risk of plummeting into the abyss. Terrorism—the absolute evil, in its contemporary form—should only be condemned. Insane, psychopathic, satanic, monstrous, inhuman, immoral, criminal: the terrorist is excluded not only from the boundaries of the law but also from the boundaries of humanity. The practice involved is illegal, the intention illegitimate, the way of fighting irregular. The terrorist neither has nor can have a recognizable political program, because politics must be conducted within the ambit of the law. However he or she acts, whatever his or her mysterious motives (or rather alibis) might be, the terrorist attacks the common good represented by the state. The terrorist represents the irrational in the face of the rationality of the state.

This is why "terrorism" is a label managed by the state; it is a term on which the state has a monopoly, just as it has a monopoly on violence. "Terrorism" is a sort of registered trademark, used in relation to a political and law enforcement strategy. Only the state can call someone a "terrorist." And, conversely, no one can apply this name to the state unless they openly declare the state's illegitimacy and compromise its sovereignty.

A "terrorist state" would be a contradiction in terms, even when terrorism originates from the state and presents itself on the stage of history as *state-sponsored terrorism*.[2] So it is preferred, where necessary, to use less prejudicial expressions, such as "terrorist regime" or "state terror," in order not to divulge the taboo that the modern state conceals within itself.

In fact politics is also always the way in which the state manages the epiphany of terror and controls its appearances before the public. The state must know not only how to maintain intact the symbols of its sovereignty but also how to manage the terror it instills in its citizens. On the other hand, terror, which is not relegated to a recondite past, remains carved into the heart of the modern democratic state; so it could always re-emerge. This is the origin of the vehemence with which the state rejects the stigma of "terrorist" for itself; this is why it reacts to terrorism with such severity.

## 2   Defusing terrorism

In order to reflect on terrorism—that paroxystic form of destruction that in its urgency is always unimaginable—it is necessary to distance oneself from the scene of horror, to step back from the violence. But this does not mean to retreat before the abject death of the helpless victims, much less to forget or forgive. Reflection imposes the need to pause in order not to be swept away by the tide of the media, by the fatal wavering between gruesome images, which elicit death wishes, and moral censure, which arouses revenge fantasies. Otherwise one would be in danger of getting into a spiral by endorsing the perverse idea of an ultimate clash between good and evil; one might end up forcing even philosophy to declare a "just war" on terror.[3]

But we must deconstruct this "trademarked name." We must defuse terrorism—all the more since the emotional charge that is inextricably connected to this phenomenon makes any such attempt difficult. We must, then, remove the bombs that are ready to explode, defuse them; but also unblock the concept by releasing it from its psycho-political trap, by liberating it from the bonds of stigma, in order to be able to explore its meaning. Only in this way will it be possible to reach a perspective different from the habitual one controlled by the state, which has a sort of monopoly on the trademark. To defuse terrorism means therefore to turn a cold, calculating gaze on the terror maintained by the state, beyond the sense of shock and dismay that it elicits.

Perhaps this is why a substantial reflection on terrorism is missing, whereas there are several historical lines of inquiry that aim to find a common thread that connects terrorism throughout various periods. But is it really possible to reconstruct a history of terrorism?

The attempts that have been made to date take at least two directions. The first is the one followed by experts like Walter Laqueur, who, beginning with his first edition of *Terrorism* in 1977, has written several volumes and has repeatedly traced a history of terrorism, inserting successive events without changing his basic approach. For Laqueur, there is no doubt: terrorism pertains only to rebels, anarchists, militants, and of course Islamists and jihadists. In his view, continuity is not even an issue, because he sees terrorism as nothing more than "the use of covert violence by a group for political ends."[4] According to this definition, any illegal act of violence would be a terrorist act. Apart from this vagueness, the definition has a much more serious limitation: it fosters a demoniacal vision of terrorism, as coming only from below. In short, Laqueur's history of terrorism is written from the point of view of the state.[5]

The second trend is the one followed by Gérard Chaliand, a specialist in geopolitics who, together with Arnaud Bin, edited a book entitled *The History of Terrorism: From Antiquity to ISIS*. In order to trace a historical line it is indispensable to recognize a persistent motive among the different forms of terrorism—all the more as the problem gets complicated when you consider both the kind of terrorism that comes from below and the one that comes from above. This is the objective of Chaliand and Blin, who declare that they are also interested in analyzing state-sponsored terrorism. The boundary between terrorism from below and terrorism from above is uncertain and fluid. The terrorist of yesterday can become the statesman of tomorrow. The names mentioned by Chaliand and Blin are Menachem Begin and Yasser Arafat, individuals who have also been used by other authors to illustrate this kind of paradoxical metamorphosis. And yet what Chaliand and Blin attempt to do is to identify a common thread in terrorism, whether it comes from below or from above—that is, in the variety of its multiple aspects, its innumerable visages. "Terrorism is above all a *tool*, or, if you wish, a *technique*."[6] Therefore terrorism is "old," at least as old as the practice of warfare. Chaliand and Blin extend the chronology of the phenomenon; they emphasize its continuity—an instrumental conception that makes it possible to trace a long history of terrorism. So what is terrorism? A tool, a technique—understood, however, only as a means to an end.

There is no doubt that this outlook has several advantages. It contributes in part to defusing terrorism by avoiding the rhetoric of stigmatization. To be more precise, it neutralizes terrorism morally, presenting it as a tool that, beyond good and evil, is neither praiseworthy nor deplorable. In fact both the members of al-Qaeda and those who fought against the Nazis in the Resistance are called terrorists; this confirms the famous dictum that someone who is a terrorist for one person is a freedom fighter for another. In this conception, condemnation can one day give way to recognition.

Besides, the search for a unifying element that underlies terrorist acts that are not only diverse but also distant in time from one another avoids the precipitous judgment on the "new terrorism" that exploded with the September 11 attacks. This judgment resounds both in the propensity to emphasize the point of rupture, as it sees that event as a unicum, and in the choice of extreme formulas such as "hyperterrorism," used by François Heisbourg.[7]

This approach has some major limitations, however. The basic thesis upon which the work of Chaliand and Blin is based is disarmingly naive, above all because it flattens out differences, reducing terrorism to a neutral technique that runs throughout history and can even boast a "prehistory." In this way of thinking, terrorism began with the Zealots, the Jews who rebelled against Roman rule—but wasn't that the first great chapter in the history of resistance? Then it continued with the Assassins, the Isma'ili sect that was active in Syria and Iran during the twelfth century and practiced political assassination. Perhaps with the intent to show the sacral genesis of terrorism, which they impute to "messianism," Chaliand and Blin maintain that "the Zealots and the Assassins are the two classic examples of a terrorist organization."[8]

Were the Assassins of the twelfth century *like* the al-Qaeda jihadists? Yes, according to Chaliand and Blin, because both are known for using so-called white weapons.[9] Seeing very different techniques as similar reaches an apex here—Chaliand and Brin put political assassination, whose target is a representative of power, on the same level as the indiscriminate massacre of civilians.[10] Thus a second limitation of this perspective emerges. In their zeal to deconstruct the terrorist strategy, to free it from stigma and censure in order to arrive at an objective definition, Chaliand and Blin end up losing sight of the political dimension. Thus the phenomenon of terrorism eludes them.

When terrorism is defused, and above all dismantled, nothing remains. It becomes impossible to grasp, to circumscribe and identify; it seems to fade away, to the point that the French political scientist Didier Bigo asserts: "Terrorism does not exist."[11] This means that there is no "concept" that can be profitably employed in the scholarly literature—because there are bombs, attacks, and people killed almost every day.

The difficulty of reconstructing a history of terrorism is connected to the dilemma of defining terrorism. While hundreds of attempts—all unsatisfactory—have been made, an adequate concept is still being sought, and in vain; in vain, because the historical forms that the phenomenon of terrorism takes are too heterogeneous and a unitary definition seems to be either forced or tautological. An example is when it is said that every act of violence that is aimed at engendering terror is terrorism.

On the other hand, the negative connotation of the term is all too evident. As Townshend has observed, "'terrorist' is a description that has almost never been voluntarily adopted by any individual or group."[12] It is not by chance that nations are the ones that use the term in the rhetoric of public discourse, calibrating the definition according to the groups they seek to delegitimize. This explains why organizations like Amnesty International prohibit the use of this label in their annual reports.

If terrorism is the result of a process of stigmatization, a psycho-political projection, then it seems debatable to trace a history of it that, besides containing anachronisms, risks above all being an ideological reconstruction. This is why, in the increasingly numerous studies on terrorism, there is a prevailing tendency to offer a political phenomenology that describes terrorist acts, along with documented historical research and a typology of the different kinds of terrorist acts.

# 3   Notes on fear, anxiety, and terror

Fear can be seen in our eyes; it can be sensed in the tight expression of our face, in the trembling of our hands. And we can feel it distinctly in ourselves—a cold feeling inside, a shiver, a spasm, but also the grip of anxiety. And yet, though everyone is familiar with fear, it is difficult to say exactly what it is. Certainly, as philosophers suggest, it is a strong emotion that suddenly arises in the face of danger, real or imagined. Contrary to what language leads us to believe, it is not the "subject" who "is afraid," but rather fear that possesses the subject, subjugating and oppressing him or her. Space contracts, time stands still. Someone assailed by fear is nailed to the spot: that person wants to flee but cannot, as if trapped in an invisible prison. Paralysis and flight: fear reigns uncontested between these two impulses. It is as if there were no way out. The body is wracked, the hands grope in vain for something to grasp onto. Fear blinds one even as one's eyes bulge out in the face of danger. Suddenly there is neither support nor refuge. The sense of familiarity with the world evaporates, trust vanishes, uncertainty takes over.

Fear is always fear of something or someone. But if the threat grows, if it spreads everywhere in a looming omnipresence, then fear loses its direction and becomes panic. On this side lies everything; beyond lies nothingness. Freed from the thing that had elicited it—the dark, imminent loss, a sudden shock—fear becomes panic or anxiety. In a famous passage of *Being and Time*, Heidegger showed how anxiety—which in German has the same name as fear, *Angst*—is the situation in which something is feared without our being able to say exactly what it is.[13] The threat is undefined. Anxiety oppresses; it makes it difficult to breathe. Once it has taken over, it is difficult to say what caused it. "What was it?" The answer is usually "I don't know, it was nothing." Anxiety is the fear of nothing—the nothingness into which the world, in its insignificance, seems to be plunged, the nothingness out of which existence constantly springs; because to exist means to emerge from nothingness, into which it is always possible to plummet again. One who suffers from anxiety is aware of one's own finiteness, of what one is not, could have been, has not been. But, owing to anxiety, one also grasps what one could be, one's own possibilities. Suddenly one is no longer at home in the world to which one belonged or had been integrated—one feels lost; but it is precisely for this reason that one is consigned to be oneself. Anxiety is a sign of authentic life. For Heidegger, the age of technology was characterized not only by the rejection of death, but also by the difficulty of giving in to anxiety.

If fear can overpower the human spirit, then it can be used to dominate other human beings. Already in the time of Machiavelli, who raised fear to the level of a political category, the close relationship between fear and power was disclosed. But being able to instill terror covertly, in order to maintain sovereignty, is a difficult art. According to Machiavelli, the prince needs to prevent fear from degenerating into hatred, which would incite his subjects to rebellion.

Fear made its entry onto the political scene with the onset of modernity. Many philosophers have examined this emotion—its uses, its potentialities. For that matter, fear of the unknown in an increasingly open world gives rise to the need for security. For Hobbes, *fear* was the basis of political order—the expedient of the *Leviathan*, which homologates the passage from individual fear to shared fear. Hobbes believed that, rather than being isolated and prey to the continual threat of a violent death, it is better, in the "war of everyone against everyone" that is the state of nature, to submit to the legitimate tyranny of a sovereign, where "terror of some power" and "terror of some punishment" will keep ties strong.[14]

Hobbes used the term *terror*, emphasizing its positive value. But it was the French word *terreur* that imposed itself in the end, in all its sinister, intimidating semantic power. If fear is despotic, terror seems to relate to an ulterior political form, where the recourse to violence exceeds all limits.

Derived from the Latin *terror*, which in turn is formed on the Indo-European root *ter-* ("to tremble"), terror seems to have many points of contact with fear. Someone who is terrified is caught between paralysis and flight, at the mercy of tremors. The phenomenonology is the same, but differences are not lacking—if only because terror is not something that can be "had" but only experienced. Terror takes over, channeling the entire repertoire of fears and strengthening them to the extreme: it is the threat par excellence. In Roman law, *terror* or *territio* [the state of being terrified] was torture. If fear has many faces, terror is the facelessness of petrified rigidity. It resembles the severed head of the Gorgon with its rolling, lifeless eyes.

What is striking is the political success to which terrorism seems destined in the modern age, a response that is not elicited by mere fear. This success is such that, written with a capital T, terror frees itself from the realm of emotions, to designate almost exclusively a new, controversial concept. It all begins when a revolution invokes it, claims it, implores its help—a dangerous relationship, which, among other disadvantages, never goes away. First it was the French Revolution that put terror "on the agenda." Thus, when we speak of "terror," we almost invariably think of revolutionary terror. How is one to judge it? Even a moderate like Kant recognized that the enormous enthusiasm sparked by revolution resides in its responding to the "moral disposition" of the human race, in which violence is relativized by that elevated design; in short, it resides in its humanity. And yet Kant spoke of "moral terrorism," by which he meant a fanatical plunge into rage.[15] But it may have been Hegel who provided the most effective definition of the political praxis of terror: "absolute, inflexible rigidity."[16] Because of terror, which is, then, an unavoidable state, abstract freedom experiences its own limitations and understands the necessity of laws; but, as that rigidity imposes itself, terror reveals its disturbing proximity to death. Terror is cold, flat death embodied in the head that is severed by the blade of the guillotine.

How could we forget these images? In later times, if terror was no longer associated with the French Revolution, this is because in the mid-nineteenth century other forms of terror took center stage, until the October Revolution in Russia and the events that followed it reproposed the theme in a new, complicated way. It would be a mistake to follow the thread of terror's political success, in an attempt to reconstruct the historical vicissitudes of terror, which, even in its rigidity, changes shape and gets transformed, throwing any kind of continuous line into doubt. The terror of the Jacobins was profoundly different from that of the terrorist attacks aimed at insurrection, as it was from the Red Terror.

During the twentieth century, it was the technique of terror as a modality of domination—but also of extermination—that prevailed. As Hannah Arendt explained, terrorism does not limit itself to eliminating the opposition; by dominating it, it becomes "total terror." In consequence, it is exercised not only on enemies but also on friends. But here lies the difference between tyranny and a totalitarian regime, which are often mixed up. In this sense, terror is "the essence of totalitarian power."[17] Here the rigidity of terror reaches a point where it is not just freedom that is suppressed, but rather any room for movement. An ironclad bond fuses the many into the one. Terror is not a tool of government— rather, terror itself is that which governs. This is what "the order of terror" means. In describing the power that devours a people—that is, its own body—and contains in itself the seeds of self-destruction, Arendt emphasized the way in which, along with its own superfluousness, terror uses for its own ends the "uprooting" of every human being. "To be uprooted means to have no place in the world."[18] But it was Horkheimer who signalled for the first time, in 1950, the danger of "a world threatened by terror."[19] This can already be read as the prelude to atmoterrorism.

Terror becomes an atmosphere. It is no longer a tool of government, nor does it govern with its ironclad order. Rather, in its apparent absence, it lets everyone be consigned to the planetary void, exposed to the cosmic abyss. No threat is necessary, because threats seem to come from the outside. The need for self-defense becomes obvious.[20] This is what occurs in post-totalitarian democracy, which therefore cannot be said to be exempt from a shared atmosphere of terror.

Uprootedness seems to be unbearable, and this is also because it has been translated into the progressive banishment of existence from the niches in which it felt protected. This is why currently terror is really the opposite of anxiety: rather than opening up authenticity, it oppresses existence, condemning it to the search for an asphyxiating, dangerous security.

# 4   Revolutionary terror is not terrorism

Although terrorism has been practiced from time immemorial, it became a protagonist on the political scene during the modern age. It was revolution that theorized it, almost as if to underline, with the prerogative of capital T, its inaugural value: Terror.

When the revolution of 1789 was put down, the defeated were immediately stigmatized as "terrorists." It was in fact in 1798 that the newly coined term "terrorism" appeared for the first time, in the *Dictionnaire de l'Académie Française*, where it was defined as a "system, a regime of terror." But already in 1795 Edmund Burke had spoken of "thousands of those hellhounds called terrorists" in his *Letters on a Regicide Peace*.[21] For that matter, the entire Thermidorian literature and the conservative pamphleteering painted the men and women of the Reign of Terror in dark hues, calling them monstrous creatures, inhuman, wild beasts thirsty for blood and relegating them to a political pathology. This was the counterrevolutionary genesis of the words "terrorism" and "terrorist." From that moment on, "terrorist" was the name of a perpetual delegitimization; it was the mark of disrepute, hurled not only at the revolutionary who, once defeated, was banished from the political scene but also, retrospectively, at the revolution itself.

Terrorism was seen as necessarily springing from Terror. Nothing could be more obvious. This dubious obviousness was reproposed, almost unanimously, by the experts. It is no surprise, then, that the equation became amplified: revolution = Terror = nihilism = totalitarianism = barbarism. This is how an elementary arithmetic functioned, and continues to function, that is the basis of both historical reconstructions and political analyses of terrorism. With regard to the former, one is even tempted to admit that we are dealing with "state terrorism."[22] And the one at fault can be none other than Robespierre. In this way of looking at the phenomenon, all the terrorisms that were to come later would be contained *in nuce* in the Reign of Terror—the ones produced from below, but also the direct heirs of the "state terror" that began with the Russian Revolution of 1917, the aberrant apogee of totalitarian terror.[23]

This confusion, belated and misleading, is aimed at eliciting a moral condemnation that reaches all the way to revolution, attacking it head-on, as if to give a warning that the mind of every revolutionary—that is, every would-be terrorist—is dominated by the impulse to kill and by a thirst

for extermination. Where does this renewed disgust for revolution come from? Did it begin with the French Revolution?
For Sophie Wahnich, author of a daring study on this subject,
there are two motives: the way in which the past is considered, starting from the history of the political catastrophes of
the twentieth century; and an idealized model of democracy
that tends to ignore its conflictual origins.[24] From this perspective, revolution appears to be the opposite of democracy
rather than its womb: a political form unto itself, as bloody
as it needs to be in order to fit under the increasingly broad
label of "totalitarianism." Thus the revolutionaries of the
French Revolution, out of love of humanity, could become
inhuman. Was blood not shed? Were the corpses of the
enemies not brutalized? The one who particularly raised these
kinds of questions was Hannah Arendt, who in her book *On
Revolution* connected the French experience to that of the
Bolsheviks.[25] According to Arendt, the French Revolution,
the archetype of an indiscriminate violence, couldn't help but
lead to totalitarian terror. Violence, certainly. But what violence, and against whom?

The French Revolution was not terroristic. Threatened
from the outside by a foreign invasion and from within by
counterrevolutionary forces, it was in grave danger only two
years after it began. In July 1792 the General Assembly had
pronounced "the country" as being "in danger," *la patrie en
danger*. Fear was increasingly widespread among the Parisian
mob. The most serious effect was the September Massacres,
when fury erupted uncontrollably. "We are terrible," said
Danton, "and we shall give the people dispensation for being
so." On March 10, 1793, the Revolutionary Tribunal was
instituted. Mottos such as "Liberty or Death" were taken
literally, while the concept of "public safety" gained ground,
in order to deal with an extreme situation. The people
demanded mass conscription in order to create a revolutionary army. On 18 Fructidor Year V—that is, September 4,
1793—the spokesmen appeared before the Assembly: "It is
time for equality to pass the sickle over everyone's head. It is
time to terrorize the conspirators. Yes! Legislators, put terror
on the agenda. Let us be the revolution." *Plaçons le terror à
l'ordre du jour. Soyons en révolution.* Robespierre, the president of the Assembly, responded: "Citizens, it is the people

who must make the revolution."[26] But the sovereign emotions of the people—as Robespierre knew well—would have to be articulated.

Contrary to what is generally believed, the Reign of Terror avoided the worst, because it permitted the legitimate violence of the populace to be restrained; it allowed its revenge to be kept in check. Raised to the level of a political method, Terror is not only a duty, but also a right. As Remo Bodei has written,

> The people and the poor did not have to withstand such impotent desperation before avenging themselves, and they did not have to endure, before rebelling, such a host of criminal actions on the part of an overbearing minority that had always enjoyed the most complete impunity![27]

Political violence, exercised publicly, ostentatiously, reaped sixteen thousand victims, all condemned by the tribunals of the Reign of Terror. Of these, 14 percent were members of the aristocracy and the clergy; another 14 percent came from the upper middle classes; and 72 percent were from the classes that had supported the revolution. The dramatist Georg Büchner, with a romantic sense of distance, had the character Danton say: "I know, I know—the Revolution is like Saturn, it devours its own children."[28] With less clamor and with a great deal of subterfuge, the monarchy had had eight thousand people killed at the Pont Neuf only a few years earlier, in 1787—not to mention the thousands who were hung in the prisons, drowned in the Seine, or executed on the wheel. But the difference lay in the "metaphysical luxury" with which the revolutionaries openly exhibited the reasons for their violence. On 9 Ventôse of Year II—that is, February 26, 1974—Saint-Just exclaimed:

> Citizens, by what illusion do you let yourselves be persuaded that you are inhuman? Your revolutionary tribunal has put three hundred scoundrels to death in a year: did the Spanish Inquisition not kill more? And great God, for what a cause![29]

Revolutionary terror strips sovereignty bare, exposing it to the open sky in a shameless manner by comparison to the political decorum that has always kept it veiled, hidden. This is why revolution horrifies the self-righteous.

If the people is the sovereign, as decided by the act of revolution, then the king cannot be the sovereign. The people does not condemn the king, it pushes him into nothingness, as required by its constitutional power. The judgment that falls upon the king like a thunderbolt is therefore not a crime. Robespierre emphasized this repeatedly, speaking of "revenge"—revenge, not justice, because the law and those who enforced it had disappeared. All that remained was the other's death and one's own self-sacrifice. Terror intervened to avoid a complete bloodbath.[30] Certainly, terror means rigidity; and the revolution, too, is in danger of freezing. But there are no other political responses. Fevered passion could devastate the body of the community, which must be able to cool down in order to constitute itself. This is, in essence, "public safety." Terror is the defense of the body of the community against what could ultimately destroy it. The revolutionaries knew, as they exercised that pure sovereign power, that they were walking on the edge of the abyss—which is not the void of nothingness but the incommensurable receptacle from which alone new forms can come to light. It is not the nihilistic nothingness, but rather the moment of nothingness—that extraordinary moment in which the people conquered sovereignty.

This is the sovereign scene described by Walter Benjamin in his essay "Critique of Violence." For Benjamin, it was impossible not to see the affinity between the violence of the people and "divine violence": *vox populi, vox dei*. This is the kind of violence that does not require sacrifice but accepts it; that does not blame and punish, but purges and expiates.[31] The violence of the French Revolution was sovereign violence.

# 5   Are terrorists nihilists?

"Nihilism" is a word that has been proliferating ever since the September 11 attacks. How else can that stupefying, destructive cruelty, for which no word seems adequate, be defined? In the October 25, 2001 edition of the *Telegraph*, the brilliant British strategist and historian John Keegan observed: "The past few weeks have introduced the world to an entirely novel threat: the nihilism of a rich and insatiable fundamentalist movement."[32]

The connection between terrorism and nihilism was again proposed by the French philosopher André Glucksmann in *Dostoïevski à Manhattan*, published in 2002. Since that time, this thesis has been supported everywhere, in an unbridled way, especially in the media. It was recently taken up by Olivier Roy in *Jihad and Death*, where, although the author distances himself from many clichés and sustains the original concept of the "Islamization of radicalism," he adds that, in this pure, non-utopian revolt, "the nihilist dimension is central."[33]

Saint-Just is not the archangel of today's terrorists. Their predecessors must be sought elsewhere, not in the public squares of the French Revolution but rather in the pages of literature—the kind of literature that described the specter of nihilism precisely when it was beginning to emerge and almost conjured it up, actually. But those who are convinced that terrorism is a form of nihilism need not turn to the great classics of literature. It is enough to consider the etymology of the word: nihilism comes from the Latin *nihil*, "nothing." This is the interpretive key, then: a terrorist is someone who believes in nothing, a non-believer or an unbeliever, for whom it would be useless to try to detect a program. A terrorist not only believes in nothing but also wants nothing. This is where his or her most unbearable crime is hidden.

Consumed by the impulse to kill, willing to teeter on the brink of the abyss, devoted to the ultimate crime, which eliminates the other simply because that other exists, the terrorist-nihilists have neither ideals nor values and know no rules or taboos. Their *ubi consistam* is limitless transgression. Their motto is "I kill, therefore I am." Always ready for the ecstasy of dereliction, they have a foretaste of the voluptuousness of the tempest even before the last, cold onslaught inspired by the joy of destruction and inflamed by the impetus of posthumous glory. Whether they call themselves agnostics or declare themselves the avenging sword of some divine will, they replace God with their own ego in order to get access to his annihilating power for at least one moment. Their only dream is to plunge the world into primordial nothingness. Their goal is to destroy, to lay waste, to reduce everything to ground zero. The lives of others hang by the thread of their own life, which they immolate in an ultimate sacrifice in order to drag with them, into eternal darkness, as many people as possible. There is no esoteric doctrine hidden in this ecstatic inebriation; rather it is a coagulation of banal, colorless passions. The terrorist's gesture can be summed up as an attempt that passes through death in order to obtain access to sovereignty.

This champion of planetary outlaws is an absolute soldier who chooses to annihilate rather than to defend, an apocalyptic artisan capable of nonchalantly transforming an airplane into a bomb, a rootless warrior capable of turning trade and communication technology into an inexhaustible arsenal of extermination. The terrorist's Kalashnikov, introduced into the space of the city, gives voice to the violence that resounds in the leaden, automatic rumble of terror. No vision of the world, no meaning guides this person's feverish actions. Self-elected to purify the world, the terrorist unleashes a senseless conflict that abolishes every frontier. Mutilated in heart, twisted in conscience, the terrorist knows neither remorse nor torment. The suffering of others does not exist for the terrorist, because others have always been outside his or her vision. The terrorist's voyage toward nothingness is an insane forward flight, an ecstatic dash toward death, a navigation beyond good and evil. The terrorist will not be able to stop before the light of destruction has sealed the darkness.

According to Glucksmann, it would be legitimate to call up a "universal alliance" against this "enemy of humanity."[34] The satanic image of the terrorist—that disconcerting acrobat of nothingness who ultimately falls outside of humanity—remains solid in reflections on the phenomenon as well as in public discourse. Beyond the risks that derive from the demonization of the adversary, this kind of partial image has the serious disadvantage of denying or ignoring the existence of a political or theological–political program on the part of the terrorist. This might be true only in some rare cases, but not for the latest versions of terrorism—unless one wants to insinuate that it is legitimate only for a state, and not for individuals, to have a program and a strategy.

The misunderstanding is deep and lies in the way nihilism is interpreted. According to this widespread conception, those who believe in nothing are stigmatized with the epithet "nihilist," which is sometimes used in place of "terrorist." But the question of whether terrorists are nihilists can be answered only after having examined the phenomenon in all of its complexity.

It is worth remembering that Nietzsche, that incomparable prophet and shrewd diagnostician of nihilism, was led to examine carefully the "illness" that afflicted his age, on the basis of the tremendous impression that the sequence of attacks in Russia and all over Europe had been made on the press and on public opinion. When in the summer of 1880 Nietzsche began to describe what a nihilist is—"the most gruesome of all guests," a sinister character who wanders throughout the house and can no longer be pushed out the door—he was almost certainly thinking not only of the protagonists of the great Russian novels but also of those obscure, inexplicable individuals who were sowing the seeds of terror on the old continent. The first of the four books into which the very controversial collection *The Will to Power* [1901] is subdivided has "European nihilism" as its theme.

The motif that was Nietzsche's point of departure is that "God is dead"—this is the "great event" that casts its long shadow everywhere.[35] The immediate effect is disorientation, loss of ideals, degradation of values. All of a sudden, the road becomes impassable. In fact one discovers that one is not moving on solid ground but on an ice pack that, as it cracks open, reveals the abyss beneath. "What does nihilism mean? *That the highest values are losing their worth*. There is no bourne, no answer to the question: 'what for?'"[36] No one is to blame for this. The nihilist is not the one who lights the spark, but rather the one who lets him- or herself be ignited, who is subject to the great seduction of nothingness. In modernity, there is a nihilist hiding inside everyone, just as the person who moves on ice represents everyone's lack of a home.

What I am now going to relate is the history of the next two centuries. I shall describe what will happen, what must necessarily happen: *the triumph of Nihilism*. This history can be written already; for necessity itself is at work in bringing it about.[37]

For Nietzsche, nihilism stands out in the full light of modernity, where it appears clearly that "[b]ecoming has been aiming at *nothing*, and has achieved nothing."[38] This is the epochal vision of the eternal recurrence that Nietzsche had in August 1881 on the shore of Lake Silvaplana. What could be more terrible than an ending that repeats itself into nonthingness? Here is nihilism fulfilled, the most extreme form of nihilism: it is "nothing (purposelessness) eternal!"[39] It would be pointless to search for traces of growth, of progress, of an order in the world that approximates happiness. On the contrary: for the existence of the individual as for that of the world, there is nothing to look forward to but the image of an hourglass that is continually turned upside down. Who could ever bear this annihilating idea? Only the "superman," according to Nietzsche—only a nihilist capable of furthering the progress of that destruction, only someone who is beyond human.

An echo of Nietzsche can be found in Heidegger, who, however, saw nihilism as a phenomenon that was not only European, but planetary. In Heidegger's view, when one is sick, one must take care to get well, even to accept what might be a long convalescence. What good would it do to rebel—as Jünger imagined, pointing to an inner parapet, a "savage land" of interiority? Better to abandon oneself to nihilism, to gather oneself into its manifestation, without presuming to stave it off—because any barrier would be too fragile, any reaction would double its power. To defuse nihilism would mean to promote its acceleration, so that nothingness would be released in all of its power, exhausting nihilism. No passage opens up "beyond the line" to signal the meridian of nihilism. It is impossible to leap beyond one's own shadow. Heidegger had no illusions; the unstoppable vortex of nihilism, making use of technology as well as of its own mechanisms, would be capable of provoking planetary catastrophes.[40] And yet one had to move forward, in the dark landscape of the rigid polar night.

For Nietzsche and even more for Heidegger, the terrorist was an extreme figure of existential, ontological, and political reaction, incapable of bearing the explosive force of nothingness, of taking it on board. Instead, the terrorist sought to dominate that power, deciding, of his or her own will, the place and time of the detonation. But in the end the terrorist's bombs are nothing more than the venting of violent, impotent rage. This character is not a nihilist; rather, rising up at the ultimate borderline, where history seems to be suffering its death throes, the terrorist seeks to cancel out the end, to exterminate it. A terrifying end is better than a terror without end. Thus this exterminating angel of a hypermodernity that is intent upon letting nothing repeat itself takes aim at the eternal return. The terrorist tries in vain to shatter the canopy of steel in which nihilism has enveloped the world.

## 6 Why defend anarchists?

But it was not German philosophy that provided the definition of "nihilist." The nihilist par excellence was born of the pen of Turgenev, who immortalized this figure in the character of Bazarov, the protagonist in his novel *Fathers and Sons*, a young physician who denies values and social order. Turgenev confessed that he had been inspired by real people of his time and by a certain attitude that he believed was already widespread. To refer to this kind of figure and attitude, he coined the word "nihilist." Its meaning is explained in a famous passage:

> "A nihilist," said Nicolai Petrovitch. "That's from the Latin *nihil*, nothing, as far as I can judge; the word must mean a man who ... accepts nothing."
> "Say, 'who respects nothing,'" put in Pavel Petrovitch [...]
> "Who regards everything from a critical point of view," observed Arkady.
> "Isn't that just the same thing?" inquired Pavel Petrovitch.
> "No, it's not the same thing. A nihilist is a man who does not bow down before any authority, who does not take any principle on faith, whatever reverence that principle may be enshrined in."[41]

Not long afterward, the term started to be widely used, with a pejorative connotation. And, contrary to Turgenev's intention (in his memoirs, he lamented the fact that the term had gone astray), it ended up becoming a tool of denunciation and condemnation, a "brand of infamy."[42]

One could stay that "nihilist" occupied the place that was subsequently taken by "terrorist," becoming therefore a synonym of "anarchist"—because anarchists are supposed to be without a principle, without *arche*; they reject authority, they combat the establishment, they negate moral values— just as nihilists do.

This semantic continuity was taken up by two literary critics: Nikolay Dobrolyubov and Dmitry Pisarev. Pisarev in particular relaunched the term "nihilist" and made the character of Bazarov into a model for every revolt. The vindication of nihilism, which would not only have a profound effect on politics but also give rise to new ways of living, found its manifesto in the novel *What Is to Be Done?* by Nicolay Chaernyshevsky, published in 1863. Premature death, condemnation, and deportation were the destiny of many of the members of the Russian intelligentsia, but this did not prevent nihilism from continuing to spread in Russia. Until that time, it had been a strictly literary phenomenon. But it was bound to explode in the city squares sooner or later.

While the transition to action was brewing in the series of attempts on the life of the tzar, a singular figure, Sergery G. Nechayev, was validating the equation nihilist = anarchist = terrorist—with effects that were going to last and prove almost indelible. Born in the Vladimir oblast, Nechayev had studied in Saint Petersburg, where he had taken part in student protests. After having spread the belief in his own arrest and subsequent escape from the Peter and Paul Fortress, in 1869 he went to Switzerland and introduced himself to Mikhail Bakunin as the exponent of a new political movement. This was the time of the publication of the famous *Catechism of a Revolutionary*, which sparked many polemics, even as to the identity of the author. Was it Bakunin or Nechayev? The answer given by Michael Confino, the historian who worked on this complicated story for many years, is certain: it was Nechayev. But this does not mean that the *Catechism* was not influenced by Bakunin who, for his part, admired the work and was fascinated by Nechayev.

The *Catechism of a Revolutionary* is a terrorist's vade mecum without precedent and remains a unicum, and not only on account of its radical nature. In its pages is condensed a philosophy of destruction and an ethical code of terror that openly overturns the formula of "thou shalt not kill" into a cold, merciless "you must kill." The rigid rules that are delineated in the *Catechism* hold for the terrorist organization as well as for its members, for the "revolutionary" whose life choice is extreme and leaves no room for changes of heart.

> The revolutionary is a doomed man. He has no personal interests, no business affairs, no emotions, no attachments, no property, and no name. Everything in him is wholly absorbed in the single thought and the single passion for revolution.[43]

Having broken all ties with the "civil world" and its laws, its customs, and its conventions, the "revolutionary" continues to live in that world *only* for the purpose "of destroying it." He detests morality because, for him, "everything that contributes to the triumph of the revolution is moral, and everything that is an obstacle to revolution is immoral and criminal." He knows only the "science of destruction." Counting only on himself, ready to undergo torture if necessary, he "passes himself off as something that he is not," for the purpose of carrying out his mission. "Hard on himself, he must be hard toward others as well." Aspiring only to destruction, he is "prepared to destroy himself and to destroy with his own hands everything that stands in the path of the revolution."[44]

Nechayev returned in 1869 to Russia, where he founded a short-lived secret organization. He killed a student named Ivan Ivanov, who had opposed his authoritarian methods, and was condemned not as a "revolutionary," but as a common criminal. The case caused an enormous uproar, one reason being that Bakunin was somehow involved.

But the relationship between Nechayev and Bakunin was plagued by misunderstandings and false steps; and it was precisely here that the dangerous and unfair equation terrorist = anarchist took hold. Nechayev *acted*—he praised action. This had attracted Bakunin to him; Bakunin could not fail to recognize the value of "destruction." But the convergence, as Bakunin himself noted at a later time, ended there.

Under the strong influence of Hegel, whose work he had studied while he was living in Germany, Bakunin developed a political philosophy of "negation," which he saw as the "only nourishment, the fundamental condition of every live life [*sic*]."[45] For Bakunin, whoever rejected the negative would end up choosing the rigidity of non-life, that is, of death; contradiction was the truth that was born of the clash between positive and negative. So for him it would have been a mistake to rid oneself of the negative, viewing it as absolute evil—indeed, this would have been a dangerous exclusion, because the negative could be transformed into an independent principle, whose effects would be ruinous. The negative should "destroy, passionately absorb the positive"; negation was the beginning of rebirth. This is why destruction and creation are inseparable, as art teaches us. This did not mean that the revolution would not be violent, but it would never take on the character of "a cold, systematic terrorism." Above all, it would be a "war against positions and things, not against human beings."[46] Bakunin criticized the ineffectiveness of terror: it was not the guillotine that had undermined the power of the French aristocracy, but rather the confiscation of its properties.

Thus Bakunin's "destruction" had very little in common with the paroxistic form of proto-terrorism represented by Nechayev that nevertheless continued to play a dominant role in the revolutionary imagination.[47]

# 7   Dostoyevsky and the terrorist inside me

The connection between terror and art, and especially between terror and literature, is much closer than one might suspect. One name is sufficient to attest to this: Dostoyevsky. Perhaps no other author has dared to immerse himself so deeply in that "wise and dread spirit, the spirit of self-destruction and non-existence."[48] Raskolnikov and the "black angel," Stavrogin, not to mention Verckhovensky, a character inspired by none other than Nechayev, and then Ivan, the atheist of *The Karamazov Brothers*: Dostoyevsky's novels teem with self-declared terrorists, but also with ambiguous "masked" characters, in which the radicalness of good—that of Prince Myshkin—is always on the point of turning into the radicalness of evil. Alyosha Karamazov, a terrorist? Why not—this is shown in Dostoyevsky's outlines and in his notebooks, especially the ones relating to the novel *Demons*.

In Russia this was the period during which the wave of attempts on the tzar's life was being hatched, fed, and directed by the revolutionary organization Narodnaya Volya, "the People's Will." The culmination came in 1881 with the assassination of Tzar Alexander II, but it also marked the end. The reason was not violent repression by the police so much as the absence of an insurrection; the assassination achieved nothing. But an exceptional literary success made up for the political defeat.

That success can be attributed above all to Dostoyevsky, who was taken up with the Nechayev affair for various reasons, some of them autobiographical. In a text written in 1873, he railed against the "nauseating" way in which the press spoke about Nechayev's followers as if they were all "idiots and fanatics." Why, he asked, should they be considered "fanatics" and "idiots"? Dostoyevsky rejected these labels, which stigmatized terrorism by reducing it to the level of a pathology.

> Yes, among the Nechaevs there can be creatures who are very shadowy, very dismal and misshapen, with a thirst for intrigue and power of most complex origins, with a passionate and pathologically premature urge to express their personalities, but why must they be "idiots"? [...] I myself am an old "Nechayevist" of old; I also stood on the scaffold condemned to death.[49]

The reference is to December 22, 1849, when Dostoyevsky and the other members of a socialist circle, having been condemned to capital punishment, were led into the Semenovskaya Square in St. Petersburg, where they waited for ten terrible minutes to be executed. But the execution was canceled and the sentence was commuted to forced labor in Siberia. In that brief span of time, as their young lives passed before their eyes, the condemned men certainly repented some of the actions they had committed, but not the ideas for which they had been declared guilty, which at that moment appeared to be "something purifying, a martyrdom that would have pardoned us much!" If anything, they subsequently changed their relationship with the people, seeking a fraternal union in shared misfortune.

I am the terrorist, the terrorist is inside me—this was Dostoyevsky's audacious gesture, which also won him the approval of Nietzsche. A "great psychologist," as Nietzsche called him, Dostoyevsky went beyond myopic moralism and had the capacity to see the basis of a crime.[50] "And therein lies the real horror: that in Russia one can commit the foulest and most villainous act without being in the least a villain! And this happens not only in Russia, but all over the world." Dostoyevsky saw this possibility in epochs of "transition," "when people's lives are being thoroughly unsettled."[51]

Dostoyevsky raised terrorism to the level of a category of the spirit, which he introjected, vindicated, even claimed. It continued to influence and ignite subsequent literature from Chekov to Conrad, from Mirbeau to Chesterton, from Philip Roth to Don DeLillo. An extreme gesture, a secret thought, an ultimate excrescence: since terrorism was unable to burst forth in flames, it found a place to breathe in literature, the space of narration, by responding to the unfulfilled promises of dull, sordid modernity.

# 8   Terror and sovereignty: on Lenin

And so we come to Lenin, that great admirer of Nechayev. How could we speak of terror without mentioning his name? Red Terror—should we impute that to him, to Trotsky, or to Stalin? It is a name associated with a betrayed revolution that arose from insurrection, surged like a wave during civil war, and was then wrecked by political policing and purges, destroyed in massacres and in gulags. At issue is the transition from "terrorist" action to state power—a decisive passage that, at the dawn of the twentieth century, not only shed light on critical events to come, but also revealed the connection between terrorism from below and terrorism from above.

So what did Lenin think about terrorism? He made no romantic concessions; he showed no tenderness or moral scruples, much less political dilettantism. Lenin made a clean break; he distanced himself from Narodnaya Volya, from a semi-anarchic past that, in spite of itself, had already marked his biography, indirectly. His older brother Aleksandr Ilyich Ulyanov was arrested along with other students even before the attempt on the life of Tzar Alexander III took place in Nevsky Prospect. During his trial, Aleksandr Ilyich took responsibility for everything and defended the right to terrorism. He was executed by hanging on May 20, 1887.

For Lenin's younger brother Vladimir, terrorist action had no value in itself; he considered it coldly, in a pragmatic context. In a brief 1906 essay that was destined to become one of the great revolutionary classics, Lenin distinguished between random war, insurrection in the old form of isolated actions that was bound to fail, and war waged against enemies who oppress the people. For him, only this last type of warfare is revolutionary, because it is not devoted to nationalistic politics; crossing boundaries, going beyond limits, it is open to an internationalist horizon. As far as the methods of fighting went, Lenin did not reject any of them. For that matter, he saw destruction as indispensable. At least in this sense, Lenin maintained a certain continuity. In his "Letter to American Workers" of August 20, 1918, he defended himself against accusations of terrorism and emphasized that "in revolutionary epochs the class struggle has always, and in every country, assumed the form of *civil war*, and civil war is inconceivable without the severest destruction, terror, and the restriction of democracy." He pointed out that the members of the bourgeoisie accused the revolutionaries of "terrorism" because they wanted to forget the "terror" that had brought them to power.

> Their servants accuse us of resorting to terror ... The British bourgeoisie have forgotten their 1793. Terror was just and legitimate when the bourgeoisie resorted to it for their own benefit against feudalism. Terror became monstrous and criminal when the workers and poor peasants dared to use it against the bourgeoisie! Terror was just and legitimate when used for the purpose of substituting one exploiting minority for another exploiting minority. Terror became monstrous and criminal when it began to be used for the purpose of overthrowing *every* exploiting minority, to be used in the interests of the vast actual majority, in the interests of the proletariat and the semi-proletariat, the working class and poor peasants![52]

One cannot say that Lenin was wrong: if a class had legitimized terror in history, it could not turn back. Nevertheless, we should not lose sight of the new way in which Lenin considered terrorism, not as a general concept but as something that took on different meanings and values. "Terrorism" can be said in many ways. During that period, Lenin was being criticized precisely for the use of terror, which some saw as a relapse into the anarchism of the century that had just come to an end. And yet, according to Lenin, the two historical situations were very different, because the protagonists were no longer a handful of conspirators but the entire working class. And one could not close one's eyes to the fact that terrorism and guerrilla warfare are transitory activities and a prelude to insurrection. Contrary to popular opinion, Lenin believed that terrorism wasn't particularly effective; on several occasions he emphasized its impotency. The biggest thing that was missing was insurrection, to which terrorism was a temporary supplement. It was a matter of passing from spontaneous action to revolutionary action, from local guerrilla warfare to general civil war.

But, once the insurrection had exploded, once the revolution had made its entrance onto the stage of history, partisan warfare, later exported under the name "guerrilla warfare," should be set aside. Otherwise it could become seditious. Terror should be assimilated to the practice and strategy of revolutionary power, becoming "mass terror." From that moment on, Lenin branded every individual terrorist act as counterrevolutionary. The revolution was still too fragile, and terror was imposed by the historical moment. Once again, and without hesitation, it was a matter of choosing between different colors of terror: white terror, which could also turn black, or else Red Terror, which was imprinted with the promise of liberation.

It was a short step from this alternative to a police state, which was instituted in Russia on November 10, 1917. The onetime saboteurs were now opposed to any sabotage: purging became routine; dictatorship made itself necessary. This had already been foreshadowed by the soviets,[53] which recognized no other power, no other laws. Dictatorship was this unlimited power. Just as there was violence and violence, there was dictatorship and dictatorship. The new order in

Russia came from the people and was exercised by the people. But for how long? Until when would terror write the history—how long before it gives the floor to liberation? Democracy had to wait...

Lenin firmly reiterated that the transition from capitalism to socialism could not happen "without coercion and without dictatorship." The weakness of the revolutionary class made a dictatorial state indispensable. It would be an "anarchist absurdity" to flirt with the idea of giving up state coercion.[54] With concentrated, unlimited power there comes to light an absolute sovereignty that can even decouple itself from its own laws and restraints. Dictatorship, understood as unlimited power, is sovereignty pushed to the extreme. It dominates through power and through a politics of power. It seeks to erase the endless horror of capitalist society by fighting against that horror-filled end that is world war—the most violent, the most reactionary form of war. This does not mean throwing down one's weapons, but rather fighting the only true revolutionary war—the war to eliminate exploitation. Was Lenin a despot? Would it be right to speak of liberticide tyranny, or perhaps to resort to the usual label of totalitarianism?

The question is quite different—above all because, for Lenin, "mass terror," sprung from individual terrorist action, was not an expedient or a strategic move. Rather it was the realization of what the first assassination attempts had had as their goal: sovereignty. And perhaps never so much as at this point in history did the close connection between terror and sovereignty come to light. The dictatorship founded by Lenin—to use the terminology employed by Carl Schmitt—was not a "commissary dictatorship." It did not suspend power temporarily but was, to all intents and purposes, a "sovereign dictatorship."[55] Although initially Lenin openly sought to find a connection with the French Revolution and to follow its model, upon close consideration he rejected this legacy, at least in part. Lenin's revolution took the opposite road, transforming terror into a state or hyperstate policy. The dividing line is the divergence between guerrilla warfare, which can presage a new chapter in history, and the kind of sovereign dictatorship that brings that chapter abruptly to an end.

This is perhaps the most relevant difference with regard to the anarchist idea, which does not fill the void with a new master and which, when faced with the abyss of sovereignty, does not erect a powerful new sovereignty but rather lets the abyss be. A politics without terror is the kind of politics that opens and spreads out around a sovereignty that is broken and has no foundation.

# 9    "Once upon a time there was a revolution"

Sergio Leone's film *Duck, You Sucker!* was produced in Italy in 1972, halfway between the dreams of 1968, which remained unrealized, and the clashes of 1977, which marked an escalation of violence. The Red Brigades had already called for "armed propaganda." In that tension-charged vigil, Leone had chosen the eloquent title *Once Upon a Time ... the Revolution* (another title by which the film is known is *A Fistful of Dynamite*) in order to relate polemically to the past the revolution that loomed in Italy's future.[56] Later on Leone had to give in and compromise with the producers, who imposed as the film's title a line taken from the screenplay.

"Duck, you sucker!"—this warning is shouted out by the story's protagonist, a former IRA fighter, to announce that a dynamite charge is about to go off. The Irishman has left behind not only Ireland but also his name, Sean. In Mexico, where he joins the revolution, he calls himself John Mallory. And yet his old name returns continually, like a refrain in the famous soundtrack of the film, composed by Ennio Morricone. "Sean, Sean"—as the indelible images from his past life pass through his mind: evolutionary militancy, friendship, love, joy, proud and serene hope. But suddenly the colors in the film become opaque and cloudy and the images blur. Sean is sitting in a pub in Ireland when all of a sudden his best friend enters, held in custody by two soldiers. His face shows signs of torture. The friend points Sean out to the soldiers with a slight nod of his head. Sean has a rifle in his hands, ready to fire. In a play of mirrors, the flashback reaches its apex. The friend once again makes an imperceptible movement of his head, this time toward Sean, as if to say: "Go ahead and kill me." Sean's past as an Irish revolutionary ends in a burst of gunfire.

What remains? "When I started to use dynamite, I still believed in many things ... in all of them; and I ended up believing only in dynamite." This is Sean's reply to Juan Miranda, the peasant bandit who, together with members of his large family, has ambushed a stagecoach. Juan cares nothing about the revolution.

> The revolution? Don't try to tell me about the revolution! I know all about revolutions and how they start! The people that read the books, they go to people that don't read the books—the poor people—and say: "Hoho! the time has come to have a change, eh!" [...] I know what I'm talking about when I'm talking about revolutions. [...] So the poor people make the change, eh... And then the people that read the books, they all sit around the big polished table and they talk and talk and talk and eat and eat and eat eh... But what has happened to the poor people? They're dead! That's your revolution... So please, don't tell me about revolutions.[57]

Like mirror images, John and Juan are destined to switch roles: with his explosives, the former IRA fighter paves the way for the petty outlaw who, swept along by revolutionary events and after having lost his children, takes on the role that history has assigned to him. It is the necessity of the moment that leads to Juan's being acclaimed as a general, in spite of himself.

Another character in the film, Doctor Villega, is devoted to the revolutionary cause. Unlike John and Juan, he believes in the revolution—indeed, he is sustained by an unshakeable ideological faith in it. He is looking forward to the new world and knows nothing about explosives. Destruction doesn't touch him, but in the end neither does death. When he is captured and tortured, he thinks nothing of giving the names of his comrades and then returning to fight for the cause. Villega represents revolution at all costs—total and totalizing revolution, which walks over dead bodies. After having repented for betraying his comrades, Villega dies on a locomotive that is hurtling like a torpedo toward another train with soldiers on board.

Three characters, three different ways of understanding revolution, three presumptive terrorists. A combination of the worst traits of each—destructiveness, criminality, blind faith—would result in the stereotypical image of the terrorist, who, in the film, is shown instead through a fragmenting, distorting prism. Once upon a time there was a revolution— in Mexico in 1913. But the film premiered in movie theaters in Italy in the early 1970s and opened with a quotation from Mao's *Little Red Book*:[58]

> A revolution is not a dinner party, or writing an essay or painting a picture, or doing embroidery; it cannot be so refined, so leisurely and gentle, so temperate, kind, courteous, restrained and magnanimous. A revolution is an insurrection, an act of violence by which one class overthrows another.

Sean, who comes from the old world, knows this very well. Unlike his two comrades—the one who has never believed, and the other who believes too much—he no longer believes in revolution. And yet his melancholy for the lost revolution, abandoned on the coast of Ireland, doesn't prevent him from taking part in other revolutions. But this time he does so only with dynamite, because the only thing he believes in any more is dynamite and its deflagrating effects. Even though he has suffered the effects of destruction—and here the words of Mao reveal their full meaning—Sean remains faithful to the power of destruction. So he puts his knowledge of explosives at the service of someone else's revolution; but not just any revolution. He can no longer play a leading role—he leaves this to Juan—because all he has retained from revolution is its dark, negative side. But he still knows how to light a fuse, mix the black powder, set the detonator. Every explosion opens up the possibility of a revolution. "Short fuse..." he comments in a decisive sequence of the film. And then he tries again. In the final analysis, Sean is a pioneer of the transition to action; he blazes the trail for someone like Juan to follow, but with an important difference by comparison to the Red Brigades or the Red Army Faction (RAF). Sean is aware that in that explosive in which his faith has found refuge there is only a potential for liberation; but it is a destructive potential that is destined to come to nothing, if an insurrection is absent. Because it is not that the men guide the revolution, but the revolution guides the men. In the final scene of the film, lighting a charge of the dynamite that he always carries on him, John blows himself up with his last cigarette.

# 10   The partisan, the guerrilla, the terrorist

To understand the role that the terrorist plays on the global political scene, it is necessary to go back to the fighters who preceded him. What affinity is there between a member of al-Qaeda and a partisan who fights to defend his or her own country?

The answer comes from Carl Schmitt, who, albeit a reactionary, acutely intuited many of the virtualities of his time. For Schmitt, politics was not circumscribed by the state, nor was it to be confused with governing or directly connected to power. He believed that the political ambit has as its differentiating mark the distinction between friend and enemy. This is a distinction that, although analogous with that between good and bad in the moral sphere and between beauty and ugliness in esthetics, maintains its own autonomy. Even if the enemy were handsome and good, that person would still be the enemy. This is why Schmitt believed that the commandment in the gospels to "love your enemies" (Matthew 5:44; Luke 6:27) was valid only in the private sphere and that the enemy was always public. The example used by Schmitt in 1932 is particularly eloquent: "Never in the thousand-year struggle between Christians and Moslems did it occur to a Christian to surrender rather than defend Europe."[59]

Schmitt believed that the distinction between friend and enemy should be an intense, extreme contraposition that takes on existential profundity. For him, politics unfolded along the trench of life, in close proximity to death, where threat looms, where sacrifice is imposed. Here war is both a presupposition and the last horizon. It is not merely the final realization of hostilities—because its goal is to kill the enemy, to annihilate the other. Rather, it is the violent revelation of the political; it is the apocalypse of politics.

Many years later, in 1963, Schmitt deepened and updated his concept of "the political" when he published *The Theory of the Partisan*. Now he recognized the new, precarious equilibrium of the world, on one side full of conflicts that World

War II had not defused, on the other pervaded by a radicalization that promised to become absolute. He concentrated
on the figure of the partisan, who not only seemed to have
emerged as a victor but also remained solidly present in the
political landscape, calling into question its order and its
principles.

The partisan is an irregular combatant. Schmitt believed
that the notion of a partisan had been born at the dawn
of modernity, when Napoleon's army, having come out of
the experiences of the French Revolution, invaded Spain.
Between 1808 and 1813, in an increasingly small area,
Spanish guerrillas—groups of irregular fighters with no real
hope of winning—fought fiercely against the French, risking
everything. In Prussia, also invaded by the French, the spark
of guerrilla warfare did not ignite. But it was in Berlin that
partisans obtained their philosophical credentials and were
legitimized. It was then that a political theory of the partisan
began to develop.

A seemingly marginal figure, outside any conventional
boundaries, the partisan undermines the law of classical
warfare, which envisions clear distinctions: between war and
peace, between combatant and noncombatant, between
enemy and common criminal. In the linear vision sustained
by this law, war is a duel between two sovereign states that
respect each other as enemies and do not criminalize each
other. Thanks to circumscribed, controlled hostilities, and
regardless of which side wins or loses, a peaceful conclusion
is the obvious end to those hostilities. In hindsight, the result
of this duel that, not without great effort, has kept absolute
enmity in check can be considered to be extraordinary.

For Schmitt, the partisan compromised the only legal war
there is—war between nations. Thus he considered the partisan to be an irregular combatant who waged war illegally
and was not entitled to rights or pity from the enemy. But
this did not mean that the partisan did not succeed in justifying his "little war," thus proving that it was not a criminal
act but rather a clash necessary for the attainment of a political goal. If the partisan was a resister who fought for liberation from oppressors, as had happened in the anticolonial
wars, he could even, in the name of his legitimate struggle,
claim a sort of legality vis-à-vis that of the sovereign state he

was fighting against. This is how a partisan could be legal and irregular at the same time.

Schmitt emphasized the difficulties of classic international law, which was forced to legalize something that was illegal. From the Regulations Concerning the Laws and Customs of War on Land of 1907 to the Geneva Convention of 1949, attempts had been made to offer legal protection to irregular combatants, especially when they were taken prisoner. If during the Nuremberg trials partisans could still pass for "bandits" or common criminals, after World War II volunteer corps and resistance movements were equated with regular combatants. But the net of international law became progressively looser, and there remained the contradiction that was destined to leave a deep crack in the *ius publicum Europaeum*: on the one hand, the attempt to remove the partisan's illegal status, and on the other the exigency not to compromise the law in doing so. For Schmitt, this contradiction signified the rupture of military order. The antithesis between regular war and irregular combat survived even after partisans became absorbed into legal normality. Subsequently other, more disruptive and more radical variants would make their entry onto the world's stage, taking the cancelation of limits and the dissolution of rights to the extreme.

Rather than defining the partisan, Schmitt traced a phenomenology of this figure, singling out four characteristics. Besides being an irregular combatant, the "partisan," as the name indicates, sympathizes with a particular party, espouses that party's cause and follows the party line. His fight is based on his political commitment. Mobility, rapidity, and surprise attacks characterize his tactics. Nevertheless, he is always attached to his own territory and is therefore assigned to a defensive position. This "telluric" characteristic was decisive for Schmitt, for whom the partisan always faced a "real" enemy—an invader, in fact; the partisan fought to protect the patch of earth where his roots had been put down.[60] The partisan did not invade foreign territory, did not cross borders, and thus the nature of his battle was national—if not nationalistic. In essence, Schmitt looked with a certain nostalgic sympathy at this figure, "the last sentinel of the earth as a not yet completely destroyed element of world history," yet someone destined to succumb.[61]

But things changed when, on account of the epochal changes introduced by modern technology, the partisan became devoted to something without limits. As partisan ties to the land became weaker, partisan ties to the party became stronger. Without being completely replaced, the national partisan struggle gave way to worldwide revolution. The autochthonous combatant was sucked back into the machinery of the technical–industrial powers. Mechanization progressively cancelled out the partisan's earthly character while increasing his or her speed, augmenting his or her mobility, and hurling him or her into the limitless thicket, into that deep, indistinct undergrowth, well beyond the limits of the conventional stage, where one fights with no holds barred against the class enemy.

The time of the guerrilla fighter whose field of activity is the entire world had arrived. How could one not think of Che Guevara, of the boldness and faith that brought him to Cuba, to Africa, and finally to Bolivia? The *guerrillero*, a "night combatant" as Che explained in his book *Guerrilla Warfare*, written in 1959 and published in Havana in 1960, was the avant-garde of liberation. This "Jesuit of warfare" was still a partisan, but one of a new type.[62] Uprooted from the earth, decoupled from the nation, this figure was committed to a political task of international proportions. Its goal was a communist revolution in all the countries of the world.

Schmitt did not distinguish clearly between these two types of partisan; and he did not call the second type a partisan but rather a "revolutionary activist," to whom he imputed "absolute enmity against an absolute enemy."[63] He saw Lenin as the true theorist of this kind of revolution—Marx and Engels seemed too abstract to him. Only a "professional revolutionary" like Lenin was capable of legitimizing the figure of the partisan, thanks to the most dangerous of weapons: philosophy. Schmitt believed that, with Lenin, the partisan took on a determining role in the history of a world that was hurtling toward the final liberation of the people.

"From Clausewitz to Lenin": this was the feature that, for Schmitt, separated war between states from revolutionary war. Lenin had understood the potential that was hidden inside someone who had fought a national civil war—a disturbing, menacing kind of military conflict—and had internationalized the partisan. In this way Lenin managed to unleash a global civil war.

This does not mean that, even after Lenin, there were not comminglings of autochthonous partisan warfare and international partisan warfare. Stalin himself resurrected the myth of the national struggle. Analogous examples include the wars waged by Ho Chi Minh in Vietnam, Fidel Castro in Cuba, and Chairman Mao in China.

From the alliance between philosophy and insurrection was born the figure of the revolutionary partisan, or rather the guerrilla, who was no longer fighting a "real" enemy but rather an "absolute" enemy. This fighter, "irregular" par excellence, knew no limits and found his own legitimacy in the negation of the existing order and in a political battle that was pushed to extreme consequences. If in classic warfare the revolutionary was relegated to a marginal role, in the global civil war he became a key historical figure.

Schmitt's vision was reactionary—it seems almost useless to say so. His flattering judgment of the autochthonous partisan was echoed in a drastic and in certain ways hostile judgment of the guerrilla. If the former defended the native soil in which he was rooted, protecting hearth and home from an invader and loyally facing a true enemy, the latter invaded and attacked another country, upsetting the partition of the earth and the sovereignty of states, undermining the law, criminalizing the enemy, and in the end being himself criminalized; the guerrilla inaugurated class warfare. Deprived of all rights, the guerrilla sought justice in enmity. And this enmity, albeit very concrete, is absolute, because it cannot be relativized or contained within limits. Anywhere in the world, under any sky, the revolutionary fights against the western capitalist, the class adversary, because it is enmity that determines the type of warfare, not the other way around.

Schmitt's portrait of the revolutionary, whose aggressiveness he repeatedly stressed, is biased and charged with rancorous resentment. One could easily rebut Schmitt's assertions, pointing out the self-sacrifice of guerrillas who are ready to give their own life to attain justice for others. Schmitt was writing when the Cold War was at its height, a period during which—as he himself pointed out—absolutely enmity was only temporarily toned down and muted. And yet his diagnosis hit the mark, above all when he pointed an accusatory finger at the radicalization of enmity and identified the revolutionary as a key figure in the age of no boundaries.

Nevertheless, we cannot fail to point out a contradiction into which Schmitt stumbled. On the one hand, he saw the revolutionary as the unquestioned protagonist, the first subject responsible for the global civil war, and on the other he saw the revolutionary as the "tool" of modern technology, singling out mechanization as the cause of the partisan's unprecedented planetary mobility. Of these two versions, however, in the end the second one seemed to prevail, particularly when, after having discussed the transformation of the guerrilla fighter—who, as a tool of the military–industrial complex, becomes a sort of technician of clandestine combat—Schmitt spoke in a premonitory, almost prophetic tone about a new type of irregular combatant looming on the horizon: the terrorist.

In the bottomless vortex of technology, in that uncontrolled, limitless whirlwind, Schmitt saw the emergence of terror and the terrifying vicious circle that accompanied it. Terror was answered with terror, in a spiral that intensified irregularity interpreted in its most disturbing form and took hostility to the extreme. The open space of terror is that of the new world order, where "a few terrorists" would be sufficient to cause a worldwide deflagration. Plastic bombs, radar devices, information networks are the new tools with which the terrorist operates. Schmitt wondered about the future effects of the pervasiveness of technology everywhere. What would happen to the irregular combatant in the age of tools of mass destruction? For those who calculate in technical terms, it would be a matter of "street police," while for Schmitt the question remained eminently philosophical even as it preserved its legal and political meaning.

In a scenario that took on planetary and interplanetary dimensions, Schmitt went so far as to advocate for a combatant capable of adapting himself to the frenzy of technology, a "cosmo-partisan" who would open up a new chapter in the world's history of destruction—because, in the age of planetary terror, as a result of the precipice of criminalization into which the two sides were pushing each other, it was possible for absolute enmity to pave the way for that annihilation to which every life unworthy of existing was destined.

Schmitt did not see the danger as residing in the means of annihilation or in the evilness of human beings, but rather in the "inescapability of a moral compulsion"[64]—almost as if, in order to remain human and not to become monsters, people were forced to make others inhuman. Thus the logic of terror would disclose all its devastating power.

Schmitt could not have known that the moral obligation about which he wrote would come to take on a religious value. European public law had arisen from the ashes of the wars of religion, and in Schmitt's time no one could have imagined that beneath the unextinguished coals there burned a flame that would erupt again, conferring an extreme intensity upon religious enmity. Although his perspective was vetero-European, nevertheless Schmitt, leaning out of the window of the future, showed rare foresight and provided an interpretive framework for reflecting upon the figure of the terrorist.

# 3

# Jihadism and Modernity

"Now, Lord, take away my life, for it is better for me to die than to live." But the Lord replied, "Is it right for you to be so angry?"

Book of Jonah 4:3–4

Had your Lord willed, all the people on earth would have believed. Do you want to force the people to become believers?

Surah 10:99, Jonah

## 1  Radicalization

In today's tormented global landscape, it is not rare for negativity to take the form of radicalization. Paradoxically, just as the world is reaching a zenith of openness, the most unexpected and inscrutable danger has arisen. The word "radicalization," which has invaded the public sphere, has condensed in it an explosive charge; it contains the seeds of the terror to come. Security measures and intelligence services, following the criteria of an unprecedented semiology of radicalization—a presumed circumstantial understanding of destructiveness—attempt to insinuate themselves electronically into this antechamber of terror in order to intercept its premonitory signs, to monitor the birth of a new human type: the "radicalized" being, sometimes also defined as "born again."

If many concepts that were formerly scattered and disconnected—concepts like extremism, fundamentalism, integralism, fanaticism—seem to have found a place in the broad field of radical activity, it is more difficult to identify the connection between terrorism and radicalization. Since there is no doubt as to the convergence of these two terms, they might appear to be synonyms. But the difference, as Farhad Khosrokhavar has explained, is in their perspectives, which are in some respects opposite, like mirror images.[1] Research on terrorism tends to focus on violent action: on the one hand, this kind of research examines the technical means that make terrorism possible and modify it throughout history, down to the use of technology as a tool for terror; on the other hand, it looks at the devastating effects of terrorism, the slaughter and massacre that are produced by it. The study of radicalization focuses instead on the agents of terror, their personal histories, the motives behind their actions, and the choices that, in a complex play of mirrors that deploys their relationship with the world, have determined their individual trajectories and the ultimate goal that has driven them to violence before they took any step to action.

Thus research into radicalization is complementary to the study of terrorism; it is a psycho-political study that has at least two advantages. The first is that it raises the decisive, otherwise elusive question as to the "why" of a terrorist's actions. What moved the terrorist to act, to the point of annihilating not only the lives of others, but even his or her own? It would be easy to speak of "fanatical delirium," "homicidal insanity," "blind terror," as happens for the most part in the frenetic circulation of news. The alternative to this facile reply, which always reduces the phenomenon to a pathology, is the way opened up by the great diagnosticians of modernity, who, beginning with Dostoyevsky and Nietzsche, have not stopped at the moral judgment of crime but instead have attempted to understand—without necessarily justifying—the motives and impulses of the radical, no matter how recondite and often unspeakable they might be. This means not only to immerse oneself in the dark recesses of the psyche of the terrorist, but also to recognize that the terrorist is still a human being, connected to other humans by a thread, even if a distressing and disconcerting one—a thread that no one can sever and that in fact becomes a chance to fathom the abyss of humanity in the age of global terror.

The second advantage of this line of research is that it examines the political aims that the media tend to leave in the shadows, or even to conceal, thus endorsing the widespread notion that the terrorists of today are nihilists. This misconception is intensified when those political goals elude the canon of traditional politics, when they cross borders, when they go outside the *nomos* of the earth, when they are revealed to be ultra-political, or even otherworldly.

The term "radicalization," with all its attachments and derivatives (one of the more recent ones being "to become radicalized") comes from the late Latin adjective *radicalis*, "having roots," and further back from the noun *radix*, "root." In this sense, radicalization designates both the process through which an individual is driven toward radicalization and the outcome of that process—that is, the fact that the individual is radicalized.

Radicalization can be said in many ways—in the present and in the past. Khosrokhavar uses the concept to make a retrospective study, particularly of European extreme left organizations, from the RAF in Germany to the Red Brigades in Italy and to Action Directe in France. Once again, it must be reiterated that, if comparisons can on the one hand bring out illuminating aspects, on the other they often lead to oversimplifications.

The novelty of the global era, otherwise ignored, is that radicalization is understood to a great degree as a putting down of roots: the desire of radicals is fulfilled thanks to a return to their roots. The extreme that used to be the goal is no longer sufficient—it must now be an extreme that springs from the very depths of a root, unshakeable and pure. In this way is reactivated the powerfully eicastic metaphor of the root—which in the ancient word stood for origins, thanks to the symbol of the tree. For that matter, we cannot fail to recall that the theme of lost roots, of a dramatic and perhaps irreparable uprootedness to which human existence is consigned in the planetary universe, runs through almost all twentieth-century philosophy, beginning with the parallel reflections of Franz Rosenzweig and Martin Heidegger. What will become of those who have been torn forever from the earth to which their every fiber seemed to connect them? In the Jews' wandering can be glimpsed everyone's exile; in countrylessness, the "destiny of the world."[2] Here we can recognize the mark left by the age of technology, the sign of incipient globalization.

The search for lost roots is a reaction to homelessness, perceived as an unjust, unacceptable destiny. This also corresponds to a radicalized person's intolerance for the unbearable burden of nothingness. The radical is not a nihilist. His or her "no," which embodies the impetuous wind of negativity, is a reactionary response to globalization whose two opposite results are the attempt to cling desperately to the earth or, in cases where the diasporic condition prevails, the attempt to put down roots in heaven. The first result is exemplified by the position of the extreme right, which, in its numerous ramifications, is by now almost more documented as defending the soil than as defending the blood. Examples include massacres like the one that Anders Behring Breivik carried out in Norway on July 22, 2011. The second result is radical Islam, which today plays a leading role on the world's stage, so much so that, in the vocabulary of the media, radicalism is equivalent to Islamism.

This depends not only on the impact that attacks of Islamist inspiration have had on western public opinion, but also on the strangeness of a form of terror that calls upon the heavens, brings God into the worldly affairs of politics, that challenges progress with its neo-archaic features, that chooses extreme forms of struggle such as martyrdom, which are repugnant to reason. Strangeness then becomes completely, overtly alien, even if the terrorist is "homegrown." On the other hand, we must recognize the Islamization of the radical revolution. There is no doubt that Islamic radicalism has, at least partly, occupied the place that in the past would have been taken by other ideologies of salvation or other programs aimed at changing the world. This is a sign of the times—or perhaps something more, because radical Islam offers both an alternative way of life, not found elsewhere, and a belonging to a

community that, albeit imaginary or virtual, asks for the
support of the "born again," of the regenerate, to bring about
a transnational utopia.

## 2   The political theology
of the planetary neocaliphate

Up until now, the terror unleashed by global jihadism has
been understood mostly as a "blind terror"—not only on
account of its destructive fury but also because of the apparent absence of a political motive. This has been the case all
the more as any exchange is impossible; the absolute weapon
of martyrdom annuls any negotiation. Hence the terrifying
image of the black-clad jihadist who, like an anomalous wave
coming from a recondite past, bursts into nonplaces of the
West such as airports, subways, and shopping centers to
reclaim his utopia, which consists of nothing.

The combatant who acted, perhaps using analogous
methods, for the sake of a concrete political goal, above all
for national independence, has given way to the terrorist, who
does not appear to have pragmatic goals. From the western
point of view, this change, which at times (in Afghanistan,
for example) takes place suddenly, with a freedom fighter's
becoming a jihadist seemingly overnight, has represented an
unprecedented caesura. If previously moral condemnation of
an act of violence could be accompanied by an understanding
of the political cause of that act, now terrorism seems senseless and insane. But the difference does not lie in the transition from a national program that can perhaps be realized to
a transnational one that is impossible to realize. Nor is the
question limited to land, because it did not change when,
after the semi-nomadic terror unleashed by al-Qaeda upon
the surface of the planet, jihadism reterritorialized itself in
part by proclaiming the existence of an "Islamic State" [ISIS].

The neo-caliphate—a sort of ideal city to which ISIS gave
birth—seems to many to be a "phantasm," the chimera of an
ideological entity founded upon a death pact; its borders are
redrawn on the map of the world every day, in the aftermath
of battles, yet its ambitions are planetary. What is in fact its

strategy, what is its political vision? The neo-caliphate purportedly has the unique advantage of being carved into the
Islamic religious imagination; it articulates the desperation of
a theology of insane hope. Beyond the desire to humiliate the
arrogant West, its goal could be summarized as one of launch-
ing a jihadist action that, with divine intervention, would
establish a universal theocracy guided by Islam. But, for the
West, this is not only a lost cause projected into an unforeseeable future; it also represents an unacceptable mixture of
theology and politics.

When we speak of political theology, even in specialized
studies, many obvious things remain in the background.
Whether the perspective is that of a synchronic tension
between theology and politics or, as happens most often, of
a genealogy of politics from theology in the sense of secularization, one remains in any case rigidly locked inside a Christianity seen through the modern eye. Both Judaism and Islam
are ignored. This confirms and tacitly approves the idea that
in the western tradition Christianity is *the* religion par
excellence—but a Christianity that has been abstracted from
its own history and given a strongly Greek character. Thus
the way of understanding the relationship between theology
and politics is Christian–modern. Saint Augustine's introduction of the separation between the "city of God" and the
"earthly city" set the stage for this way of seeing the relationship between theology and politics. It is not only that there
seems to be no doubt about this separation, but any presence
of religion in the public sphere is judged to be an illegitimate
intrusion. Politics must emancipate itself from religion: this
is the motto of the secular thinking that, in its most extreme
version, becomes laicism.[3] All this is possible because Christianity, giving up (albeit not definitively) many of its prerogatives, agreed to submit to political power already from the
time of Constantine the Great, and recognize its sovereignty.
The *cives* (citizens) bent down, the faithful awaited justice in
the next life.

The situation is different with Judaism and Islam, which
are not *only* religions. The separation between theology and
politics cannot be anything but fiction, just as the projection
of categories of modern Christianity is forced and short-
sighted. Hidden here is a profound motive of conflict in the

current context, because this projection impedes the ability not only to see the peculiarities of other religious traditions, but also to perceive their different phases and to understand the themes that are the order of the day.

What has been the relationship between theology and politics in Islam, and what is it today? How should the gesture with which the neo-caliphate was inaugurated be interpreted? We often hear talk about "political Islam," by which is meant the entrance of the Islamic religion onto the political scene, harbinger of every evil. But, if we look closely, politics has never been separated from religion in the Muslim world. If we exclude the period of Mohammed's preaching and perhaps that of some of his immediate successors, this rule has been in place for centuries, up until the Ottoman Empire. An essential and binding foundation of law, that is, of the sharia, Islamic religion subordinated itself to the temporal power of the caliph, the malik, the sultan, the emir. The emir, although he presented himself in the guise of "commander of the believers," never exercised any religious duty; this was entrusted instead to the Sunni *ulama* and the Sciite mullahs. It was an internal balance difficult to maintain, but it was also a clearly delineated theological–political relationship. Thus one cannot speak of a "theocracy" in the Muslim world, although this had always been the ultimate ideal of Judaism.

During the twentieth century, several particularly traumatic historical events caused an implosion of that balance in the Islamic world. In 1924 the caliphate was abolished, while the western powers broke up the Ottoman Empire. For the first time the Islamic world lost its theological–political sovereignty. General Kemal Atatürk embraced the western principle of the nation—in Arabic, this word was translated with *watan*, which previously signified "native"—and he severed ties with the *ummah*, the Muslim community, eliminating the caliphate. The founding, in Turkey, of the first secular state in the Islamic world, in a relation of mutual exclusion with Islamic theology, was a double affront: it proved that the political order could do without the sharia, and it removed God from his position of authority in the public sphere. The caesura was deep, because Islam underwent the separation of political sovereignty from the community of believers—but the West did not grasp the gravity of the situation. And subsequently, during the anticolonial struggles, the tension between citizenship of a nation and Muslim brotherhood remained. It is impossible to understand the Islamist movements of today without taking into consideration this still open wound. The first Islamist organization, the Muslim Brotherhood, appeared in 1928.

But it was the Iranian revolution of 1979 that truly marked a definitive turn. The relationship between theology and politics changed—it was turned upside down through an innovation that brought an ayatollah to power. A religious figure became the leader of a nation-state. Thus was born a hybrid political form that had no precedent in Islamic tradition; it would be a mistake to define as a theocracy a regime ruled by religious leaders, given that it is really a hierocracy. Similarly, one should not speak of a theocracy with regard to Saudi Arabia, which is rather a hereditary monarchy that follows Wahhabism, an austere Sunni religious movement.

In Afghanistan, which was torn by conflict and bloody internal struggles, the Taliban took power in 1996 and inaugurated the Islamic emirate guided by Mullah Omar. Iconoclastic fury was unleashed. In spite of appeals from international organizations and protests from all over the entire world, the two giant statues of the Buddha in the Valley of Bamiyan were pulverized with an immense charge of dynamite. On March 19, 2001, the television channel Qatar Al-Jazeera broadcast images of the devastation. According to the strictest rules of Wahhabism, which requires that the sharia be followed literally, works of art dating from before the advent of Islam must be eliminated. The same happened later at Palmyra. But it would be reductivist to interpret that explosion, which aroused intense outrage in the western public, as no more than an extremist outcome of a superstitious aversion to images. If idols were destroyed; if women were forced to wear the burqa so that their faces and bodies would not send dangerous messages of desire; if the flying of kites, which used to soar happily through the skies over Kabul, was banned; if owning birds as pets was prohibited, since their song might distract the faithful from the study of the Quran; if all the signs that could distract attention from the unrepresentability of God were forbidden—well, this was in order to present God's sovereignty every day, always and everywhere. Already during the emirate, which lasted for five years, politics had been reduced to being a tool of theology.

A further, decisive step was achieved on June 29, 2014, when Abu Bakr al-Baghdadi proclaimed the Islamic State, presenting himself as the caliph, the vicar of the Prophet, with the intention of reconstructing the original Islamic community. Based upon the strictest sharia, ISIS is the latest and most radical form of Islamism, the utopia of a complete failure of a political system that gives way to theology. But the latter is understood as *logos*, the discourse of God in the sense that it is God himself who speaks—through his works, but also through his punishments. This is the origin of the extreme explosion of the unlimited sovereignty of God through cruel acts and brutal savagery. In fact, under this form of Islamism, it becomes necessary to enact the absolute power of God, intended to instill fear to the point of terrifying his creatures. This kind of sovereignty cannot be circumscribed within a territory or a state, which can only be thought of as a temporary base of operations; one must take off from this base in order to impose and expose that sovereignty everywhere. According to the strategy developed by the neocaliphate and defined in a text published in 2004, it is necessary to spread terror around the world, to sow the seeds of chaos, to "manage brutality," destroying all institutions.[4] This would be the prelude to establishing, here and now, the Kingdom of God.

This radical utopia, in its three forms—the Sciite and, later, the two Sunni forms—is anti-political, or rather ultra-political, because it is founded on a delegitimization of politics, considered corrupt and unclean, and aims to surpass it through religion. This is why it is a mistake to speak of "political Islam," thinking of a politicization of religion. The attempts, past and present, to leave politics behind in order to restore the sovereignty of God through the purity of the Muslim religion, different as they might be, are all based upon the same fundamental conception of Islamism. It is not inaccurate to say that "Islamism"—a term that appeared, not by chance, at the end of the eighteenth century—is the Muslim response to modernity, which arrived with Napoleon's troops in Alexandria, Egypt in July 1798. Islamism landed in Egypt with cannon fire, pushing forward through the power of technology; from the arsenal of the Enlightenment it unloaded two concepts, that of civilization and that of nation, which were intended to foster a political strategy that followed the rules of reason. This was the first face-to-face encounter between the West, which presented itself as "advanced," and the East, which was taken to be "despotic." Many other encounters would follow, up until the period of anticolonial struggles. If initially the concept of a nation seemed to gain ground, subsequently the Muslim world rose up, also as a result of the disintegration of the *ummah*. Islamism is the reaction to western modernity; it is the revindication of the roots of Islam, in a resistance centered above all on the Quran. In this sense, Islamism is the ultra-Islam that, in order to immunize itself, sets in motion all its antibodies to defend its identity; it redoubles, it intensifies to the point of turning shame into honor, humiliation into superior integrity. It succeeds in deriving religious hope— albeit only in the world beyond—from the memory of past wounds. Since it is the outcome of a traumatic "transition to the West," Islamism—unimaginable without the categories of modernity, which it confronts and in which it is articulated, at least in part, even as it rejects them—is, to all intents and purposes, postmodern.

The neocaliphate of Abu Bakr al-Baghdadi therefore has a long history, and the theories to which it harks back are not new. Perhaps the writer Tahar Ben Jelloun is right when he says that the precise date of its origin is August 29, 1966, the day when the Egyptian President Nasser had Sayyid Qutb executed by hanging.[5] At that time, the writings in the Quran were not yet being used as a weapon of terror; in many Arab countries, from Syria to Iraq, a form of secular socialism was spreading.

But who was Qutb? Largely unknown not only to the western public but also to the circle of philosophers, Qutb was the theorist of radical Islamism. This complicated, tormented figure cannot be reduced merely to that of a militant. Born in a village in southern Egypt in 1906, after he finished university Qutb devoted himself to poetry and literature and attained a certain fame as a polemicist. After a failed romance that made him remain celibate for the rest of his life, in 1948 he went to America, where he was supposed to stay for some

time, studying the educational system. That experience
affected him profoundly. The American way of life seemed
to him to be primitive and banal, materialistic and immoral.
When he returned to Egypt after two years, he abandoned
his more moderate positions and began to organize the
Muslim Brotherhood. It was during this period that he wrote
*Social Justice in Islam*. The program of brutal authoritarian
modernization instituted by Nasser after the *coup d'état* of
1952 provided the background for Qutb's life and thought.
Arrested in 1954 for propaganda against the Nasser regime,
tortured and condemned to 25 years of forced labor in the
camp at Tura, Qutb devoted himself to writing, among many
other things, his monumental 30-volume *In the Shade of the
Quran*.[6]

Outb's criticism of modernity, which he saw as also going
through a break with a Muslim tradition that had been
plunged into the darkness of unbelief and ignorance, cul-
minated in the principle of *hakimiyya*, the "sovereignty of
God," which he believed should be reestablished in the world
at any price, even that of violence. The jihad—the holy war—
rose to the level of an obligation, an imperative as strong as
the "five pillars" of Islam. In order to develop the concept of
jihad, Qutb, breaking with a secular interpretation, turned to
the doctrine of Ibn Taymiyya, a theologian who lived from
1263 to 1328.

Why in the world a medieval theologian? Why did Qutb
adopt this untimely authority? Today Taymiyya is a point of
reference for the Salafist movement, particularly the jihadists,
both because he called for the most radical jihad and because
he maintained that human politics was illegitimate and that
there was no place for it in Islam, given that only God had
the right to govern.

Qutb in his turn reproposed the idea of a jidad directed
both internally, at the Muslim world, against corrupt people
and apostates, and externally, at suppressing every human
power and restoring sovereignty to divine law, *shari'at Allah*.
From this perspective, the most illegitimate sovereignty would
be that of the democratic state, where the people declares
itself to be sovereign on the basis of a contract. Qutb's criticism of the western conception of statehood was combined
with a project of deterritorialization that ignored any borders

and aimed at God's universal sovereignty. This was the project of an absolute theocracy, realized in the *ummah* and entrusted to a revolutionary avant-garde that, thanks to jihad, would wipe out all the previous ideologies and institutions. In this vision, strongly heretical with regard to traditional Islam (in which, for that matter, the influence of the revolutionary movements of the time was evident), jihad takes on the form of a cosmic conflict, a metaphysical battle that can only end in the ultimate victory—the unlimited sovereignty of God.

Neither of the self-proclaimed disciples of Qutb—Osama bin Laden and the new caliph, Abu Bakr al-Baghdadi—has achieved the prestige that Qutb enjoyed and continues to enjoy in contemporary Islamism.

# 3   The postmodern horsemen of the Apocalypse

They follow the mirage of an imaginary neo-*ummah*, the mythical community that stands out, homogeneous and solid, in the whole and dazzling past that inflames their oneiric visions. But they do not live in the past. They flee from the asphyxiating present in order to project themselves backward, toward remote times, and return to the tomorrow that looms ahead. While they inhabit the virtual reality of the McMondo, they ride powerful steeds, galloping across the desert of the seventh century; they listen to the ancient calls of jihad; they flirt with the rise of Wahhabism during the eighteenth century, becoming intoxicated with the overwhelming, perverse images of ultraliberals. Ostensibly neo-archaic, they counter the American dream with an epos of fairy tales and heroism. Obsessed with their distant enemy across the Atlantic and with the enemy of the Near East before that, these are the postmodern horsemen of the Apocalypse.

The end of the world is imminent; the signs of the last moment are obvious: this is the certainty that arouses the fervor of the jihadists of today. Their inspiration is not the traditional exegesis of the Quran, which is reluctant to translate the idea of the end of times into the crude, precise language of reality. Rather the source of their eschatology, the idea of what will happen at the extreme limit, just before everything plunges into the abyss, is, paradoxically, a text from the New Testament, the Apocalypse [Book of Revelation] of Saint John (13–17). Using biblical symbols and prophetic references, the text speaks of the fall of Babylon, the corrupt metropolis, advocates the annihilation of pagan nations and the triumph of the just, but, above all, alludes in enigmatic words to the final conflict that will come to pass between the coming of the Antichrist, announced by false portents, and the Second Coming of the Messiah.

For centuries, even from its classic beginnings, this vision has nurtured Islamic apocalyptic literature, which in its most recent, most extreme versions has led to the incandescence of jihadism. The spasmodic wait for a turning point in history, for an event capable of changing its course, of sounding the moment of retaliation, had been a mass phenomenon in the Muslim world for decades. A turning point came in 1979, the year of the Khomeini revolution in Iran and of the Soviet invasion of Afghanistan, but also of the attack on Mecca, in the heart of the Grand Mosque, by some three hundred insurgents who, guided by a powerful family from Najd, proclaimed that the Redeemer of Islam had arrived.

Efforts were redoubled to read the unmistakable signs of the definitive downfall of the *jahiliyya*, the pre-Islamic age of darkness, in the sequence of events that straddled the twentieth century and the twenty-first—from the victory of the Taliban to the destruction of the Twin Towers. But it was above all the war in Iraq, unleashed in 2003 by the United States with the support of British troops—an occupation that was lived as a "new crusade"—that sparked an increase in apocalyptic literature; and the latter became more and more incendiary. It would not be reckless to speak of a real "apocalypse of terror."[7]

It was predicted that the black-clad disciples of the Mahdi, the messianic figure of the redeemer, would descend from central Asia, cross through Iran, and then head toward Syria, to arrive at last in Jerusalem.[8]

A caliphate destined to unify Islam had already been prophesied several years earlier. But the proclamation of the "Islamic State of Iraq and the Levant" took everyone by surprise. For some analysts, this was the most significant event since the Six-Day War. ISIS represented a surprise—and not just a strategic one—even for the jihadists; and it reinforced their millenary convictions. This explains the extreme violence that the jihadists have demonstrated on many occasions. The coalition of 60 countries that came together in a worldwide effort against ISIS is gigantic, yet impotent against adversaries who are prepared to fight against the Antichrist, Al-Masih ad-Jahal, the "impostor Messiah," in a total, no-holds-barred war with no possibility of a truce, up to the final victory. This is a battle fought to the extreme, one where there is no front line but only the border between good and evil.

The eschatological clash can take place anywhere on the planet; the jihadist apocalypse is by necessity planetary. This esoteric view of history and its course concentrates on the present deciphered according to a Manichaean schema, an extremely simplified reading that does not require the study of texts or a knowledge of tradition. This is why the jihadists are neither fundamentalists nor traditionalists. On the contrary, they are accelerators of conflagration. They keep an impatient vigil, watching for the signs that will reveal the end, convinced that they belong to an initiatory avant-garde that holds the key to decrypting a hidden meaning that others cannot see. They believe that they can see hidden intentions, sinister plots, impenetrable, destructive conspiracies that lie behind events. The tumult of actuality and the certainty that they are on the right side of history are sufficient for these lieutenants of the Apocalypse, whose ranks can be multiplied through rudimentary enlisting. Thanks to its esoteric, apocalyptic reach, global jihadism is able to function without a hierarchical organization; it can follow the horizontal, diffused model illustrated by Deleuze's "rhizome," becoming the violent jihad that is unleashed at close quarters.

# 4   The path to terror

Life was always the same in the third-floor apartment in the large block of flats on the outskirts of the city. Between the glass and the concrete, the roots of any plants had dried up long ago. Everything there spoke of exile: the cold neon lights on the boulevard below; the screech of the streetcars heading into the center of town; the figures of the neighbors, familiar yet strangers; the garish sign on the supermarket across the street. Here and there in the corners of the living room there was an antique pitcher, a pair of pipes, some old photos that gave a glimpse into a past that had been lost—the past of the parents, and of the parents' parents. Among the faded photos there was the image of an old man, who in spite of his clearly failing health exuded a sense of dignity.

Wouldn't that life have been happier? The question is pointless. The father and the mother had decided to pull up roots and emigrate, to seek their fortune elsewhere and ensure a better future for their children. But that future seemed to have no horizon. And in the meantime there surfaced all the hardships and indignities of that decision, which to the children seemed to have been a senseless betrayal of their origins. They were victims of a genealogical amputation, a denial of their identity that had been carried out by their parents, those assassins of their own origins—and yet it was the children who had to pay a very high price for that. They no longer felt at home anywhere—not in the desolate present, not in the irremediably lost past, not in a future that seemed to be forever postponed.

Certainly they had the freedom of an emancipated life, of which the generations before them could only have dreamed. And yet that freedom had become a burden to them, the constriction of a lasting choice that they did not feel up to, for which they did not have resources. They could mold their own existence without having to bend to constrictive rules, without the chains of a tradition. The assortment of choices was vast, like the merchandise in a department store. But it was precisely this that caused confusion, restlessness, and a feeling of being lost.

There was nothing reassuring, nothing that offered support either inside or outside the home. There was not even the shadow of a community anywhere: at school, at the gym, in the corners of the park, on the anonymous streets of their multicultural neighborhood—a place with no history and no character. It was impossible to find a refuge. In the distance there was the mosque. But for these children of emigration, for these rootless orphans, even that religious universe was mostly detached and unknown. Strangers, outsiders consigned to fragmentary, discontinuous relationships, condemned to repeated frustration, to a mortifying, incomprehensible humiliation, they came up against a myriad of closed doors that exacerbated their struggle and intensified their desperation. They felt rejected without knowing why, mercilessly discriminated against even as they had to endure all that crisis of identity. They felt victims twice over—both of the useless concessions that their family had made to a cruel and inhuman society and of the marginalization that disturbed them so deeply. Shame merged with wounded pride, in an explosive combination that produced rage above all else.

The rootless orphan on his way to being radicalized can affiliate with a group in order to feel that he belongs at least there, or can seek comfort in a virtual community where he forges new alliances, makes contact on Facebook or Twitter with like-minded others, with people who think and feel as he does. Then his perception of himself begins to change, as he realizes that his condition as a "victim" is shared by others, by the group, by the virtual community. The boundaries around victimization grow larger. He puts together images he has seen online or on television, images that foster his radicalization by proxy. He identifies with the Palestinian, the Chechen, the Iraqi, the Syrian... He is not the only one who has endured wrongs. This was how, in a process of radicalization by proxy, two brothers of Chechen origin, Tamerlan and Dzhokhar Tsarnaev, came to plan and carry out the terrorist attack on the Boston Marathon in April 2013.

But radicalization does not always involve a transition to violent action. The pledge to "make them pay" can be deferred or expressed in other ways. Rarely, however, does this kind of rage get channeled into traditional politics, which for adolescents is an obscure, inaccessible sector of the paradise inhabited by famous people. The question is no longer one of changing the world, but one of leaving it—but not without having attempted to better their own condition. In the absence of other alternatives, the two opposite paths that can be taken are delinquency and religious conversion.

A chaotic journey characterized by wounded dignity and an exacerbated sense of exclusion can lead in the first place to aggression toward those who are seen as "enemies"—agents of the state, symbols of social success or of a "normal" life—and after that to delinquency. Excess becomes the figure of ordinariness, violence is perpetrated without any remorse by those who feel themselves to be victims; brutality governs their relationship with all their fellow citizens, as if the social contract of non-belligerence had been suspended. An ecstatic dimension of existence prevails: the ecstasy of drugs, but also the ecstasy that pushes one to go beyond limits, to go increasingly too far, even at the risk of losing one's life. Rather than accepting unsteady, poorly paid work and having to follow rules that impede access to consumer goods and reduce one to insignificance, one can attempt to strike, to take what is there but is inaccessible, thumbing one's nose at a society in which one is nothing more than a despised intruder. If the motto is "I consume, therefore I am," the desire to consume becomes a way to ask for the recognition of one's own existence—but in the transgression of delinquency, which, besides being guided by egoistical motives, remains part and parcel of the society it purportedly rejects.

The path to religious conversion, which is masterfully described by John Updike in his novel *Terrorist*,[9] is the mirror image of this. This is the story of Ahmad Mulloy Ashmawy. Trapped in the unshakeable rigor nurtured in a mosque of New Prospect in New Jersey under the guidance of a Yemeni imam, Ahmad spirals into a violence from which there is no return. Apathy and depression give way to ardor, to being inspired by God, which takes the form of an ecstatic fulfillment and of an exaltation that spurns the world and all the people in it. The one who has been excluded now excludes; the one who has been despised despises that corrupt world enslaved to money, to sex, to appearances.

The spasmodic search for lost roots, the struggle to regain an identity is irreducibly unique for every young terrorist. A trifling incident can start him or her down the path: some insinuating remarks made on a street corner by a friend; the charismatic influence of a fellow inmate; the huge amount of material available online, written for disciples with hardly any knowledge of Islamic theology and law, which anyone can download from jihadist websites. For western law enforcement, indoctrination is not a crime. A message on WhatsApp, a photo on Instagram, an exchange of chat messages—and the neophyte enters into the virtual community of potential jihadists.

The first step toward radicalization is a rebirth: being "born again." This holds true for converts but also for those who find another Islam, one that is very different from the Islam of their own families.[10] The generation gap becomes a definitive caesura. Almost all radical Islamists are, or feel that they are, orphans. They can forge only horizontal ties, usually by strengthening the connection between brothers. Kouachi, Abdesalam, Abaaud, Benladghem, Aggad, Dahmani, Bakrouli, Abrini—the number of brothers who have dedicated themselves together to terrorism is striking. It is not by chance that the new name given to terrorists when they are initiated often begins with Abu—Abu Ali, Abu Salah, and so on—which means "father of." The son declares himself to be a father; he becomes his own progenitor and gives life to an imaginary posterity. But he also takes on board the past, regenerating his parents, attempting to convert them, or promising to save them through his sacrifice.

Radicalization is a process of regeneration, healing, purification, expiation. In this asceticism of repentance, a separation is accomplished from the unjust, corrupt, hypocritical world—a separation that promises well-being and salvation, recovered, according to one of the etymologies of the word *Islam*, once a danger has been averted.

That insignificant, dreary apartment in the large building at the crossroads to nowhere, in the uncomfortable suburbs, suddenly becomes a springboard toward transcendence, the headquarters of revenge and retribution. Anguish is calmed, depression gives way to exultation; a life on the brink of shattering rises to a new fullness of being. The new name calls a new person to life.[11] Whether this newness remains hidden from the public space or is marked by explicit signs, the chosen man has an unaccustomed and unknown perception of himself as he acquires dignity, a sense of superiority, and pride, which had been denied to him. His resentment seems to fade, while his rage, thanks to his chosen status, becomes sacred. Violence takes on a different meaning. One who is already outside the law may remain there, in the name of a law that is greater and more just: the law of God. The small-time criminal finds retribution in his unconditional sacrifice to a noble, higher cause. Transposition into the religious register transforms his hatred for that corrupt world that has rejected him into an indefectible sense of superiority, which condemns him to accept the role of the negative hero. In the oneiric universe that he now inhabits and where he becomes the spokesman for the imaginary community that has chosen him, the avenger of oppressed Islam accepts his negative recognition. If others do not respect him, they must at least fear him, see him as a threat, a scourge that imposes itself on them with terror. He finds his homeland in the neo-*ummah* to come, which he will never see in this life but to which he can witness through his own death.

## 5   Cyberterrorism

Just as technology is both an opportunity and a threat, so is the Internet not only a technology of liberation but also a tool capable of spreading, increasing, and magnifying violence. All the terrorism of today, beyond the "media jihad," would be unimaginable without cyberspace. This space is neither completely public—because it does not have the effective openness of real space, with its horizon, its unpredictability, its deep, inaccessible corners—nor totally private—because it lacks secrecy although it is sectarian and continually attracts people who are connected by shared convictions.

Midway between public and private, between the real and the oneiric, the Internet offers the individual, lost in the anonymity of modernity and exposed to the unprecedented openness of a globalized world, the alternative of a welcoming community. This person finally feels accepted, belonging to something intimate and supportive, strengthened in his or her convictions, reinforced in his or her intuitions. Existence acquires meaning, takes on a well-defined and increasingly unambiguous direction. A rapid online exploration of videos, posts, articles, speeches, testimonies—a voyage that might have taken months of research in earlier days and would have been granted only to a few—reinforces the searcher's vision of the world, which, seen from the Web, looks like a universe easy to master. Space is condensed; time is compressed; one's identity is defined and protected behind a trench erected against an enemy who is only virtual to begin with.

This applies all the more to those who are in the process of becoming radical. Their farewell to the environment that surrounds them is rendered possible by the Web, which contributes to delegitimizing traditional institutions—the family, school, academia, the old political parties—but also religion, deprived of its exegetic, philosophical, and legal richness. Easy access to texts that have been concocted by an enterprising jihadist intelligentsia, available also in English, has enabled an entire generation to circumvent long years of study and to make use of a code limited to a few precepts, an Islam reduced to the letter, often in a Salafi version.[12] Entrance into jihadist websites and then active participation are only a short step away. The incendiary message is simple: war to the bitter end against the corrupt, unclean world, against the West, symbol of every evil.

But the jihadist Internet is only in appearance a salvific community: rather than opening up new scenarios and offering new perspectives, it soon turns out to be a cage. After propaganda comes recruiting. The content, limited to video clips at the beginning, transits easily to sites where heroic warriors are shown engaged in bloody battles with enemies whom they put to death, annihilating them in a few motions. Explosions, carnage, decapitations—the new disciple becomes accustomed to violence, gets used to cruelty, acquiring a foretaste, so to speak, of the homicidal task that awaits him or her in an international metropolis or on the battlefields of Syria and Iraq. Looking at these sites begins as a pastime, almost a game; one enters the fray with innocuous, imperceptible steps, ignoring the real consequences. Between reality and fiction, the online jihadist becomes accustomed to death in the abstract, to death without a face; is trained to keep an emotional distance, which the computer screen guarantees; practices by cutting and pasting images and fantasizes about reproducing them in the world and in history. Far from being a simulacrum, the apocalypse seems to him to be within reach. Managed in a flexible way, in decentralized forms and without a hierarchical structure, the virtual community of the jihad makes each one of its members autonomous; each one has a license to kill and is called upon to be the protagonist of the next terrorist attack. The transition to action is fostered by the Web, which by its virtual nature does not have the sense of the non-real; rather it indicates the premise and the promise of a reality to come, that intoxicating scenario that after having experienced it on his computer screen, the jihadist recruit pledges to translate into reality.

## 6   Jihadist thanatopolitics

Perhaps more than anywhere else, the connection between terror and modernity emerges in the concept of "holy death." A name that corresponds to the disturbing enormity of this act of suicide-homicide has not yet been found. Why kill yourself in order to kill? But also why kill in order to kill yourself?

Recourse to the absolute weapon of one's own death, amplified by sensationalization from the media, unleashes a catastrophic planetary process. In the age of hypertechnical weapons, that definitive act of death is impossible to reciprocate—it is the apex of asymmetrical terrorism. And yet this explanation is partial and biased, because it considers the outcome without shedding light on the phenomenon in all its complex psychopolitical genealogy.

To deal quickly with the question, one might speak of "suicide bombers," as is usually done, or even of "kamikazes," a term capable of indicating the exotic provenance of the threat, so alien that it oversteps not only what is civilized but also what is human. This would find confirmation in the well-known reward of the voluptuous virgins in heaven to which Allah's martyr, this archaic intruder into the enlightened global landscape, is supposed to aspire and in which he purportedly believed even before he was reborn.[13]

Upon close inspection, the gesture of one who accepts death in order to kill is part of what could be called "thanatopolitics," as Roberto Esposito has suggested. Thanatopolitics is the effect of a modernity in a state of decomposition, the result of an autoimmune disease in which one protects life by negating it, in a deadly, paradoxical nexus that is laid bare by the act of suicide-homicide.[14]

And yet the novelty of jihadist thanatopolitics, which is without precedent in the history of human self-destruction, resides in the furious desire to anticipate the apocalypse, which is slow in coming, in an uncontainable will to precipitate the end of time, in a febrile activity that wants to produce catastrophe rather than wait for it to happen, in a a desperate aspiration for a worldwide neo-*ummah*—that third dream, turned to annihilating the degenerate and arrogant western world, a mirage that disappears in the vortex of negation to the point that the means becomes the end, forgetful of life, and in the explosion of lacerated corpses, in the massacre of dissolving flesh, death—symbol of lost sovereignty—achieves a sovereign triumph.

The figure of the suicide attacker stands out, in its modernity, against the background of a long tradition to which it seemingly aspires to hark back, but from which it is separated in a decisive way. And it is this separation, often ignored, that should be clarified.

Martyrdom has a long history in monotheistic religions, beginning with Judaism, where Qiddush Hashem—the sanctification of the name of God—was required in extreme situations, for example in order not to submit to idolatry or commit murder. The martyr, who testified to the name of God through his sacrifice, is therefore called *qadosh*, holy. Here there is no trace of heroism, much less of pleasure. The martyr dies because he has no alternative. And he faces an anonymous, inglorious death, as in Hitler's gas chambers. The history of Jewish martyrdom, studded with dates—70, 135, 1096, 1349, 1492, 1648—reached its apex in 1942–5. As Daniel Boyarin has shown in his book *Dying for God*, Christian martyrdom, which reached a pinnacle in the first centuries CE, was closely connected to Jewish martyrdom.[15] The Christian martyrs scandalized imperial Rome, where the choice to be a *martyr*,[16] to testify to the one God, was a source of incredulity when not one of anger, not least on account of the effects it had on proselytes. Over time, however, the dividing line between death accepted as a condemnation and death coveted for the sake of leaving this vain world and obtaining salvation in the one beyond became more fluid. And yet the martyr's rush toward death could no longer cross the line into suicide, which is forbidden by both the Jewish and Christian religions—because, as Saint Augustine wrote, "certainly he who kills himself is a homicide."[17]

In Islam, the figure of the martyr, the *shahid*, stands midway between the saint and the hero. In the Quran, the word *shahada* means testimony. Only later, also because of the influence of the Christian martyrs, did "dying in the cause of God," *fi sabilillah* (Quran III, 151), take on the value of a sacred death that attests to the authenticity of the martyr's faith. But the *shahid* not only defends himself, dying in the struggle against the infidels. In Islam, martyrdom is "offensive" in nature.[18] As is said in the surah "Repentance," "They fight in the cause of Allah, so they kill and are killed" (Quran 9.111). Responding with violence is legitimate. It would be unthinkable to turn the other cheek, in conformity with the ideal of non-resistance that passes from the Old Testament— "He giveth his cheek to him that smiteth him" (Lamentations 3:30)—into the New—"whosoever shall smite thee on thy right cheek, turn to him the other also" (Matthew 5:39). The *shahid* fights and, whether he wins or succumbs as a martyr, in either case he will be recompensed. The difference lies in the relationship that links martyrdom to jihad, in all its meanings, in the Islamic tradition: from the believer's inner commitment to a fight with himself, in order not to transgress, to the war against the external enemy, the infidel—a challenge that predisposes the believer toward the supreme sacrifice. The two versions have coexisted over the centuries; at times the accent could be placed on one rather than the other. And it is not a foregone conclusion that the mystical effort of the martyr on the road to God should not culminate in abnegation through martyrdom. In Sunni Islam, the martyr is one who immolates himself in the process of carrying out jihad; in Shia Islam, he has the characteristics of one who succumbs to death and is later memorialized in a cult of sorrow.[19]

With different nuances, the martyr is an integral part of Islam. But the figure of the candidate for a holy death is new, coming onto the stage of world history with dramatic vehemence during the Islamic Revolution, and therefore in the conflict between Iran and Iraq. The factory that produces martyrs is not on the battlefield; the way was paved for it by the theological–political reflections of Morteza Motahhari

and Ali Shariati, who humanized the image of the imam
Husayn, grandson of the Prophet Muhammad and leading
character in the Shia pantheon, brutally slain in the Karbala
massacre in 610. Exponent of a militant form of Shia Islam
with traces of Marxism, Shariati portrayed Husayn as a revolutionary, an example both to the *mujahid* (the combatant)
and to the martyr, who accepts death when everything is lost.
"If you can, kill; if you can't, die!" The martyr steps in when
defeat is inevitable, when the only thing left is to sacrifice his
or her own life while taking away the lives of others.

But what is the reason for this final gesture? The reason is
not only that the combatant does not renounce violence
against the enemy, but also to testify to the legitimacy of his
cause in the future. The martyr is the "heart of history." In
this revolutionary eschatology, the radical act of martyrdom
acquires a disruptive political and existential value, which
marks its distance from the religious tradition to which,
however, it continues to look back. Shariati was the philosopher who gave voice to the new generations in their encounter
with western modernity, to which they aspired, but by which
they felt rejected. The new martyrdom became the expression
of a double impossibility: the impossibility of fulfilling oneself
and the impossibility of keeping up with an enemy who was
too strong. If traditionally martyrdom was the exception, in
modernity it is the norm, accessible to everyone and carved
onto the body of the community; it is the paradoxical itiner-
ary along which the individual finds fulfillment in death.

The first to use their own lives as weapons and their deaths
as messages of terror were the very young Iranian martyrs of
the early 1980s who, wearing the "keys to paradise" around
their necks, ran straight into Iraqi machine-gun fire. It was a
massacre the likes of which had not been seen since the Battle
of Flanders during World War I. But that wave of adolescents
who rushed into the face of death seemed to upset any sense
of logic. The Iraqi soldiers fled in order not to go insane. And
yet that sacrifice did not have any strategic result.

Iran's Islamic Revolutionary Guards, to help their Shia
brothers, exported this kind of martyrdom to Lebanon, where
Hezbollah, the "party of God," was then forming. The means
were perfected, the strategies were refined. The first suicide
attempts, which took place in Beirut and Tyre in 1982 and

1983, disrupted Middle Eastern geopolitics. Crossing the frontier between Shia and Sunni, the new weapon was adopted by the Palestinians in their conflict with Israel. Then this form of martyrdom began to branch out across five continents, from Kashmir to Chechnya, from Sri Lanka to Turkey.

In the twenty-first century human bombs have erupted in western metropolises, and the use of this absolute weapon has taken on unforeseen dimensions everywhere, becoming in the end a recurrent event. The globalization of holy death is the seal that terror has put upon our age.

How is it possible to fight for a better life by destroying oneself? What sense does it make to immolate oneself for a better world, if one leaves the world by sacrificing oneself? The suicide attacker strikes a deep blow on western reason and imagination. The causes are numerous—some more obvious, others more recondite and unspoken. First and foremost, being confronted by someone who is ready to die for a personal cause incites fear and anxiety; for a long time, this possibility was cancelled out not only by the value placed on life, but also because no cause seemed any longer to merit such a sacrifice. Not to mention the suicide attacker's relationship with death, which is completely different from ours, if not opposite: on the one hand, that closeness to death, which becomes almost a daily relationship, and the search for posthumous immortality; on the other, an obsessive avoidance of death, which is eliminated from the sphere of life, rejected through a perennial "not yet," defied in a race toward eternal youth that embodies the sick postmodern dream of immortality.

It is not only a matter of suicide, which has always simultaneously disturbed and fascinated the western tradition; nor is it about the risk that the action will be imitated, an effect known at least since Goethe's *The Sorrows of Young Werther*. And it is not just about the choice of dragging others along into one's death either—morally repugnant as that might be. What is most disturbing is the blatantness of an action that takes on political significance and becomes a new weapon, which, in its unnerving starkness, takes by surprise a world that believed it was super-protected by technological weapons. But someone who doesn't necessarily want to survive cannot be threatened by any weapon. The very logic of power is based on the fear of death—above all the power exercised by the state, which purportedly has a monopoly on violence and the implicit threat of death. But what can the state do against someone who inflicts the gravest punishment upon himself or herself? Logic is thwarted, security disappears, power appears in all of its impotence.

The black-clad attacker is there, on the pavement at Istanbul airport, already wounded. It is the evening of June 28, 2016. Shots have been fired into the crowd of travelers, gunfire has been exchanged with the security forces. A vigilante cautiously approaches, gun in hand; but suddenly he flees. A few seconds, transmitted immediately by media outlets all over the world. Then, with a gesture that is at once epic and ignoble, the terrorist uses his own body as a weapon. It is as if the screen were shattered, covered with blood and lacerated flesh.

It impossible to look away; and the questions come fast and furious. Why did he do it? What did he think before detonating his explosive belt? Was he assailed by doubts, struck by remorse? Did hesitation hold him back for a few moments? Did the face of the one whom he wanted to avenge suddenly appear before him? Did he say to himself that he could no longer bear living? Did he think that God, whose name he had invoked earlier, would reward him for having served him with the ultimate sacrifice? Did he want to kill himself in order to kill, or to kill in order to be killed?

These questions are destined to remain unanswered. It would be impossible to know in each case how suicide was sublimated into personal sacrifice, where the desire to annihilate oneself overlaps with the desire to destroy.

The neo-martyr appears as the mirror image, in reverse, of the *homo sacer* delineated by Agamben.[20] If *homo sacer* can be killed but not sacrificed, the neo-martyr can be sacrificed but not killed.

Both in videos and in written texts, the new martyrs claim as their own this condition achieved through death and beyond death, signing their last will and testament with the words *ash-shaheed al hayy*, "the living martyr." Often to this signature is appended this verse: "Think not of those who are slain in Allah's way as dead. Nay, they live, finding their sustenance in the presence of their Lord" (Quran 3:169).

Attacks on sovereignty have the paradoxical result of a way of living only through dying. If one cannot take one's own life away from sovereignty, one can at least take away one's own death. Sovereign only over the *eschaton*, at the final limit of life, where life passes into being its opposite, the neo-martyr gives himself or herself to death, the creator of a life that otherwise would be worthless. The neo-martyr's self-affirmation consists in self-negation.

In this thanatopolitics, death, absolving the martyr from the duty to protect life, triumphs as the supreme finality. And that triumph is shared by the neo-martyr. The impotence of life is answered by the power of death, increased tenfold. The suicide bombing is charged with symbolism. The attacker's lacerated, destroyed body is a symbol both of life on earth, devoid of dignity, and of sovereignty, shattered and destroyed.

And yet, precisely apropos of his revindication, we must distinguish between on the one hand the martyrdom that still fits within a national cause (Palestinian, Kurdish, Chechen, Tamil, etc.) for the sake of which, in a war that continues to take more traditional forms, the body of the martyr is destroyed, pulverized, as it represents the negated space, the cut roots, the lost "fatherland"; and on the other hand the martyrdom that calls for global jihad. The latter is not trying to reclaim territory; it does not face a clearly identified enemy; and, above all, it is not a fight for a circumscribed political goal. Since the beginning of the twenty-first century, the neo-martyr, with surprise attacks and dreaded incursions, has become the protagonist of terror and immolates himself or herself for an ultra-political vision, a transnational neo-*ummah*. Although there are plenty of aspects that the two types share and that have intensified to the point of parox-ysm, the neo-martyr type has traits of its own.

This figure springs from modernity, even though the neo-martyr is opposed to modernity. In this sense neo-martyrs take their distance from tradition, of which they are nonethe-less radical exponents; they also take their distance from their own religious foundations, which they often ignore, elude, disregard. Their death is already problematic. Is it a suicide in disguise, which would be forbidden by Islam (as by any other religion), given that only God can take a life? Or is it a sacrifice in defense of Islam, which is being threatened by a powerful enemy? In that case, it would be a legitimate jihad. Discussions on this topic are heated. What is certain is that neo-martyrs challenge not only political sovereignty, but also religious sovereignty. In an ambivalent relationship in which they crown themselves with a prestige that they usually do not have, neo-martyrs harken back to tradition while undermining it, and it frequently happens that religious authorities, giving in to compromise, issue theological edicts, *fatwa*, aimed at legitimizing martyrdom.

Islam crystalizes the rejection of western modernity. This rejection is born of a transition to the West that is to a large degree completed. Even though they present themselves as warriors of the desert, neo-martyrs are in reality westernized Muslims who have already experienced exile; they know what it is to be lost in international cities like New York, Berlin, Los Angeles, Paris, Rome, or London; they have been condemned to anonymity, contempt, and indifference in the metropolises that on the one hand offer privileged access to modernity, on the other push you away into total isolation. Behind the opulence on display in shopwindows lurks the poverty to which most are doomed, a poverty made more unbearable by an undeservedly fragmented existence. Modernity is an emperor with no clothes, exposed in it most repugnant aspects; the American dream translates into an impossible consumerism. The West rises up in all of its negativity. Malaise is projected outward in an absolute evil that must be combatted. Clash of civilizations? This is difficult to sustain. This is rather the case of a westernized individual who declares war on the myth of the West, which the neo-martyr feels excluded from and therefore demonizes.

Lack of access to modernity, a profound sense of not belonging, weariness of being oneself, and an urgent need for affirmation provoke a definitive break. In a Manichean universe that, having abandoned the thousand blinding colors of the postmodern supermarket, is divided into black and white, sacred and profane, what is permitted and what is forbidden, western civilization, the realm of anomy, is opposed by a new *ummah*, drawn from mythical roots and projected into a phantasmatic future. This planetary neo-*ummah*, formed on the Web as an alternative to the capitalistic global village, becomes the new monolithic virtual fatherland of the jihadist, that archeofuturist who can attribute everything that is negative—arrogance, depravity, thirst for power—to the West, and everything that is positive to the neo-*ummah*, which will never betray him or her.

In the near term, adherence to jihad gives life meaning; it offers dignity and the ability to overcome the impotence to which the neo-martyr felt relegated. All his or her energies are mobilized in an inflexible antagonism, sealed by metaphysical hatred for a faceless enemy, a disembodied icon from the Web. And it is in the dark labyrinth of the Web that the jihadist prepares, in turn, for death. Impersonal and evanescent, digital death makes real death seem indistinct and insignificant.

Executioners who cannot be executed except by God, to whom they openly appeal, almost as if that cry of *Allahu akbar* could legitimize them as the right hand of God, neo-martyrs are ready to kill whatever is western in themselves even before they kill whatever is western before their eyes, in the certainty that the end of time is at hand and that their actions will accelerate the apocalypse. A final gesture—and in the resulting explosion the neo-martyr dissolves into the neo-*ummah* of an immemorial future.

# 7   Media, new media, and terror

Besides being the effect of a sort of auto-immunization that protects life by negating it, besides expressing a furious desire to hasten an apocalypse that is slow in coming, jihadist thanatopolitics leverages a terror that is sensationalized by the media. This is where we can grasp the decisive characteristic that distinguishes jihadist thanatopolitics from the thanatopolitics of the Nazis, which was no less apocalyptic. Following the motto *Nacht und Nebel*, "Night and Fog," the Nazis carried out a program of terror while concealing and denying it until it was carried out.

Contemporary terrorism, in all its forms, thrives on publicity because it addresses public opinion, directly or indirectly. It seeks out a public stage where the eyes of the world can reach; thus it enters into a tacit, unconfessable alliance with the media. If in the past vengeful terrorism had already conceived of action as a means of propaganda, there can be no doubt that the escalation of terrorism has proceeded hand in hand with the development of modern means of communication. After the great print outlets, a decisive role was played by radio and television, and now by the infosphere of the Web.

What is called "terrorism" is what the media choose to show. The alliance between terrorism and the media resides in a bond of reciprocity that can no longer be severed, because that would contradict the laws of entertainment. The terrorists produce the traumatic event and the media simply sell it. They could choose not to do so, adopting the only "anti-terrorist measure" that would perhaps be capable of having some success: silence. In this way terrorist attacks would be deprived of their sensationalistic impact. But that would violate the duty of the media to provide information, aside from the fact that a concerted, solid silence would be unthinkable in the age of global media. What is called terrorism is a phenomenon inscribed in the current public sphere—pervaded, managed, and narrated by the new media. In addition to the Web, satellite television, with its live transmission of images, has made terrorism global. Without it, the large media outlets that address the international public, disseminating information in a continuous stream—CNN, CBS, Fox, but also Al-Jazeera—would no longer have sensational new events to present as "breaking news." Enslaved to their audience, coerced by competition, subject to the hard precepts of the market, these outlets are the most faithful and devoted allies of global terror. The video cameras are already on site, or ready to arrive in a few moments, to the point of determining in advance where the theater of terror will be. In this regard, Baudrillard has stated that "the media are always on the scene in advance of terrorist violence"[21]—as if they had made an appointment ahead of time. For their part, the terrorists try to choose places that are suitable for their telegenic explosions. While the satellite outlets ensure that an event will be covered, the terrorists themselves seek out media coverage, skillfully exploiting the powerful technical capabilities of western media.

Much more than any conquest of territory, it is the invasion of the infosphere that has sealed the success of terrorism.

The more unprecedented, more spectacular, more merciless the attack, the greater the guarantee of its success in the media. For that matter, even a minimal incursion is enough to have repercussions throughout the entire system. The media outlets transmit live images to the tireless consumers of terror, who are always awaiting news that will interrupt the boring, pedestrian television programs that fill part of their normal life. All of a sudden, the television audience increases thanks to the marketing of emotions and the morbid fascination that connects the agent of terror with his or her audience. How could this connection ever be broken? The alliance of terrorism with the media also brings to light the affinity that today's terrorism has with the neoliberal arts of the stock market. Thus any discussion of the "war on terror" becomes all the more hypocritical.

The obligation of the media to disseminate information enables terrorism to get itself talked about. The chains of reciprocal blackmail are very strong, and will probably be so for a long time. But this is always about making a demonstration of power. By now, terrorist events are treated according to a habitual schema, whereby the image is accompanied by a stream of news and followed by analysis and commentary. While the print press, less dependent on images, now has the task of providing critical analysis, the satellite channels, which broadcast live, set the agenda, in addition to having exclusive rights to images. The immediate effect of this situation is an emotional way of treating news, such that sensationalism is enhanced through the use of worn-out, hackneyed phrases that in the end equalize and decontextualize any event, impeding any deeper reflection. A paradoxical approach has emerged of late: the idea is to forbid speaking about the goals of terrorist actions in order not to become a sounding board for ISIS, for example—as if that were sufficient to break the perverse alliance. But this only reinforces the conviction that terrorism is a temporary pathology.

Setting the agenda means choosing which event to cover and which one to ignore. An event that CNN doesn't cover is not even considered to be a "fact." The narrative created by the media articulates reality and constructs the palimpsest of terror. But not all terrorist attacks are considered equal by the media. The violence perpetrated by Boko Haram, the

Islamist state in West Africa, on June 17, 2016 in a refugee camp in northeast Nigeria resulted in 18 women being killed. But it received only a few minutes of news coverage and was forgotten the next day. It is easy to imagine how many terrorist attacks do not even reach the dignity of the television screen and are consigned to blacked-out information, and perhaps also to the darkness of history. Only marginal space was given to the terrorist attack that took place in Beirut on November 12, 2015, by comparison to the attacks that took place in Paris the next day. It seems inevitable that, for the western media (as for the public, for that matter), there should be different ranks of "humanity."

Although violence is spreading everywhere in brutal, bloody ways, terrorist attacks make a particular impression on account of the dramatic display of violence, which always renders the event symbolic, albeit in different ways. The agent of terror does not propose to obtain only a concrete objective; well beyond that, he wants to garner attention as a vehicle for a cluster of meanings, and to intensify the effect of terror. Raymond Aron understood this when he wrote in 1962 that an action can be called "terrorist" when its psychological effects are far greater than its purely physical results.[22] The more scenically symbolic, the greater the impact and the more powerful the message. For this reason, every terrorist act should be interpreted in its symbolic rituality.

The symbolism of terrorist acts can reside in their date—for example June 14, the French national holiday, for the 2016 attack in Nice; or in the means used—often the airplane, symbol of economic vitality; or in the types of buildings that are targeted, such as abortion clinics in the United States, museums and resorts in Tunisia, or hotels in Egypt, chosen so as to affect tourism. The targets can be information systems—those networks of power, if only in cyberspace, attacked by hackers—or commercial centers, metropolitan areas, discotheques—places that until recent years were the pride of the society of well-being. On account of their symbolic weight, the attacks of September 11, 2001 were not only dramatic acts of violence, but also a spectacular drama.

How can acts of violence be transmitted in the media? This political as well as ethical question becomes extremely acute when images are involved. It was not by chance that the eyes of the television cameras were closed before the dismembered or charred corpses of the victims of the September 11 attacks. Western media, albeit with some differences, do not show violence in all its nudity, in its macabre obscenity, which could foster a pornography of disaster. The violence presented by the media is, then, a sort of cosmetic spectacle, made appropriate and suitable for the public, almost innocuous. But isn't this a form of censorship? Exercising control to the point of a news blackout? These kinds of questions have sparked debate between those who, like Baudrillard, warned against the danger of inebriation through images, which can cause addiction and replace reality, and those who, like Susan Sontag, argued that it is necessary to show images for their ethical value, their ability to involve viewers and make them feel responsible when faced with the suffering of others.[23]

This debate, along with the theme of sensationalized violence, has been partially superseded by the emergence of new technologies and the ruthless use to which they lend themselves. This has marked a decisive turn for terrorism, which is to some degree freed from its complicity with traditional media. If a camera from a satellite outlet is not available, the alternative is the Web. Videos can be posted on YouTube, photos can be posted on Instagram, propaganda websites can be set up by anyone.

A case that aroused profound indignation, and not only in France, was the massacre perpetrated upon the Ozar Hatorah Jewish day school in Toulouse by Mohammed Merah. A present-day Herostratus who craved notoriety, Merah filmed all the phases of his attacks with a GoPro camera strapped to his body, including the moment when he killed three Jewish children in the schoolyard in cold blood. Merah sent the video to Al-Jazeera, which, after some hesitation, refused to disseminate it. Communication via the Web is not limited to increasing the impact of a terrorist act; it also becomes a continuation of the terror by other means.

In a universe where closed-circuit security cameras and cell phones are everywhere, the windows that look onto terror have multiplied to the point of amplifying its traumatic effect, so that everyone is now a sort of survivor in a state of shock; the power of planetary terror is immeasurably increased. Blind violence and the desire to exhibit it distinguish this kind of terrorism from earlier forms of destruction, which sought to cover up the traces of crime. Starting with the encomium of a "media jihad" woven by Ayman al-Zawahiri, the ideologue of al-Qaeda, in 2003, the jihadosphere has never stopped disseminating scenes of massacres, executions, decapitations, crucifixions, burnings, and stonings, making them a decisive propaganda tool.

The neo-caliphate even has its own media agencies, including the Al-Hayat Media Center for the outside world, as well as its own experts in mastering the new digital weapons of terror. Enough material exists to create a substantial media archive, taking into consideration not just the corpus of multilingual publications but especially the large number of videos.[24]

Against the backdrop of the dazzling blue of the sky, the glaring ocher of the desert, or the leaden blue of the sea—on one side are the victims to be sacrificed, in orange jumpsuits reminiscent of Guantánamo, while on the other side are the executioners in their black uniforms, with no indication of rank or hierarchy, who prepare with hieratic gestures to carry out the ritual. The digital caliphate produces cinematically directed videos and sends them, with no filter, to their western enemy.

# 8   The car bomb

Atmoterrorism, radio terrorism, bioterrorism, cyberterrorism: these are the specters of technical extermination that, along with nuclear extermination—the specter of all specters—agitate the present and disturb the future. One day in the not-too-distant future, the two great threats of the twenty-first century—global terrorism and the unstoppable proliferation of weapons of mass destruction—could converge in a diabolical alliance, producing one last explosion and putting the final seal on human history.

But the relationship between terrorism and technology is more paradoxical than one might imagine. And while weapons of mass destruction—from nerve gas to netwar—have risen to the status of abstract icons of the postmodern strategic imagination, another weapon—more simple and more concrete—has become the explosive vehicle of the metropolitan terrorist mechanism: the car bomb.

When was the car bomb used for the first time? How did this ingenious, lethal technique evolve? In a compelling book, Mike Davis has traced the genealogy of the car bomb, which, from its earliest days to today, has proven to be "the poor man's air force."[25]

The noon bell had just sounded when Mario Buda, the avenging angel of the Italian anarchists, made his way through the crowds of Wall Street. At the corner of the street, in front of J. P. Morgan & Company, he left a horse-drawn cart. Subsequently flyers demanding the release of political prisoners were found a few blocks away. It was September 16, 1920. Nicola Sacco and Bartolomeo Vanzetti had been arrested a few months before. Stolen dynamite, cast-iron sash weights, and an old nag: these were the ingredients with which Buda assembled his "infernal machine," unleashing unprecedented terror in the temple of American capitalism. The cart became a huge mass of fire; Wall Street was gutted by a gigantic crater as a dense cloud of smoke enveloped the skyscrapers. Forty people were killed and more than two hundred were injured. All that was left on the sidewalk was the horse's head, a shattered hoof, and some twisted iron. Buda managed to flee to Italy and was never captured.

Buda's idea was taken up by a group of Catalan anarchist union members who, on April 24, 1921, in Barcelona, the "city of bombs," stole a taxi and filled it with explosives. But the taxi crashed into a street lamp and the attempt failed. A few years later, in 1927, Andrew Kehoe, a farmer from Michigan who was up to his ears in debt, vented his frustration on his fellow citizens by blowing up a school. At the beginning of the 1930s, the "infernal machine" was again used for political motives against the dictator Machado in Havana, where that terrorist model had been imported from Barcelona. Apart from a few improvised attempts, the concept of the car bomb—of using an anonymous vehicle that could pass unobserved and detonate its load of explosives near the intended target—was a staple of the modern political scene until January 12, 1947, when the Stern Gang[26] drove a truckload of explosives into a British police station in Haifa.

From that time on, in a singular, uninterrupted chain reaction that provoked multiple counterattacks, the wandering car bomb spread from one end of the globe to the other.

Vietnam, Ireland, the United States, Lebanon, Jordan, Egypt, Sri Lanka, Italy, Cechnya, Peru, Colombia, India, Thailand, Kenya, Nigeria, Turkey, Serbia, Spain, France, Great Britain—the list could go on and on. There is no longer any corner of the planet that has remained immune, as the curve of car bombs has grown exponentially. Like an "implacable virus," the car bomb is part of the DNA of today's world. One might say that it has become almost as global as the iPod.[27] While it has taken root in the cracks of ethnic and religious hostility and prospered in the deserts of inequality and in the slums of resentment, the "infernal machine" has found its home especially in urban centers and metropolises, where it has left a long trail of death and destruction. From Belfast to Damascus, from Bogotá to Palermo, from New York to London, the car bomb has made its way, opening up craters in cities all over the planet. Since the invasion of Iraq in 2003, Baghdad has become a global factory for car bombs, even competing with Kabul, which for a long time held this sad primacy. Initially an exclusive trademark of Hezbollah, truck bombs spread more widely later on, especially in the Middle East, and then broke violently into Europe.

The flexibility of using a vehicle has to do not only with the load of explosives, but also with the fact that the vehicle itself is adaptable. The driver can abandon the vehicle before the explosion, or can stay with it until the very end; different types of vehicles, including trucks and vans, can be used; sophisticated explosives or synthetic fertilizer can be employed, or explosives can even be done without altogether. In short, the ease with which the ingredients as well as the instructions for building a bomb can be obtained explains how this method has spread all over the world—it offers equal opportunities to all and sundry. And the transfer of information and know-how has a history of its own.

An invisible weapon, endowed with a surprising potential for destruction, capable of making a great deal of noise and thus offering a vast, incontestable echo of the terror it creates, the car bomb is an inexpensive tool, suitable for use in attacks that are relatively simple to plan and carry out—attacks that can result in large numbers of casualties and are destined to stain their often anonymous perpetrators with the blood of innocent victims. Davis defines the car bomb as "inherently fascist," returning to the figure of that father of car bombers, Mario Buda, who purportedly became a follower of Mussolini after his return to Italy.[28] Perhaps Buda's horse-drawn cart represents the pinnacle of age-old anarchical fantasies, which aspired to blow up kings, tyrants, and plutocrats. Through a series of perverse metamorphoses that gave birth to a monster fed by innumerable massacres and aroused by short-sighted strategies, the sequence of wandering bombs, which goes from 1920 to the present day, runs parallel to the sequence [sc. of assassination attempts] from 1878 to 1932 and beyond. Parallel and yet distant, because it has little in common with gestures, albeit violent, such as that of Ivan Kalyayev, who aborted his first attempt on the life of the Grand Duke Sergei Alexandrovich when he saw that the Grand Duke's wife and two young nephews were in the carriage with him. In his 1949 play Les Justes, Albert Camus evoked these revolutionaries of tzarist Russia without idealizing them: they, and those who continued their legacy, never followed the logic of blind terror.

By contrast, contemporary terrorism, which is blind and yet craves visibility, strikes indiscriminately, making use of a do-it-yourself arsenal, thanks also to hybrid technologies— for example, car bomb plus cell phone plus Internet. This is what happened in the massacres in Paris on November 13, 2015, where the use of various technologies made it possible to synchronize explosions in several locations, without a hierarchy and without orders from above. Just as the Web has made the new terrorists independent of the media, so has the avatar of the car bomb, in its many and at times extremely simple forms, become a technical superpower: if on the one hand it has led technical experts to speak of a "fourth-generation" strategy and to admit their own impotence, on the other hand it reveals the perilous flexibility of the globalized world, which is the true weapon of mass destruction.

# 9   Explosions, massacres, decapitations

Lacerated corpses, scraps of flesh, charred human remains, fragments of a human body that exploded in order to make others explode. This is more than simply murder, because the person who carried out the act intended to dismember his victims, to disfigure their physical uniqueness, to destroy their dignity. After the slaughter, nothing is recognizable any more, nothing can be put back together—so much so that not only the identification of the corpses, but even burial becomes painful, almost impossible. There seems to be no trace of humanity in that unwatchable spectacle where bodies are mixed together, where the limbs of victims and executioner are often interchangeable. Sometimes, while the abdomen of the suicide bomber has been pulverized by his explosive belt, his head remains intact. The effect of disgust and repugnance is deliberate; it is part of the terror.

But massacres have taken place throughout history. Humanity is humanity. So why should we be so shocked? In the end, what is the difference between the cadavers produced by a terrorist attack and those burned to death by incendiary bombs? Images of a distant world, made even more distant by the filter of television or computer screens, suddenly become reality. The savagery of mass killings has entered into the metropolises of the world. This is what is so disturbing— because the unwritten law of modernity prohibits manifestly savage acts in public spaces. As Elias Canetti wrote: "Today it would be harder to condemn one man publicly to be burnt at the stake than to unleash a world war."[29]

Terrorism breaks this unwritten law, brutally taking the stage. The kinds of massacres that used to be confined to cities with exotic names like Kabul or Baghdad, Mosul or Aleppo—slaughters treated as fires yet to be put out, hotbeds of untamed savagery—these break out nowadays in the heart of western cities. Life is no longer what it used to be. Emergency measures put into effect by the authorities cannot allay the anxiety that is everywhere. Dismay and fear, insecurity and anguish alternate in a crescendo that keeps pace with the orgy of annihilation that continues to spread. Terror exceeds every limit.

Is it possible, in peacetime, to be mowed down by a Kalashnikov while sitting at a table in a café? To succumb to the blows of a hatchet while riding a high-speed train? In a world that was never armed as it is now, the passerby, usually destined to disappear into indifference, can suddenly turn into a completely hostile soldier, a planetary outlaw ready to eliminate anyone who lives within a certain perimeter, under the motto "I kill, therefore I am." Since there is no front line, any place can be a battlefield: an open-air market, a train station, a university campus, a tourist village, a restaurant, an embassy, a church, a beach, a school building, an airport, a disco, a shopping center. Terrorism aims at creating a demonstrative, almost self-celebratory sort of violence that needs a stage on which to play out—a stage that will have resonance in the media. So places that used to be spaces of conviviality have now become places of high risk.

Once the perimeter of action has been circumscribed, the terrorist flaunts his destructive power by proclaiming himself to be sovereign within that fatal zone. Under the banner of asymmetry, the terrorist does not truly enter into combat but brings along the atrocity of war without respecting its rules, shows no regard for anyone because the attack is total, not selective, and resorts to the weapon of summary punishment, condemning the victims to a humiliating, anonymous death, which the principle of "whoever" and the idea that everyone is interchangeable make even more senseless.

Shots fired at random, horrified screams: the homicidal fury strikes without previous notice and does not wait for a reply. Whether acting alone or with others, the terrorist has the goal to kill suddenly. Unlike in torture, here the violence is immediate.[30] Hand-to-hand combat gives way to cold metal, which penetrates the defenseless nakedness of the flesh. Whether it is long-nurtured hatred, clear-eyed conviction, rage, depression, fanaticism, or a craving for revenge, family traumas or conflicts—the motives are mixed and confused and no explanation is plausible, because every story has its own characteristics. Perhaps this is why only writers have dared to trace the emotions and thoughts of the protagonists of such crimes. At one with their automatic weapon, whose crackle seems to relieve them of any weight, to free them from the chains of guilt and morality, the terrorists almost fuse with the violence, which carries them into the vortex of absolute freedom. They kill for the sake of killing, while even fear of their own death diminishes. Their self dilates, their body diameter expands as they destroy the world around them— until, in an ecstatic dance, they leave behind, in triumph, even their own being.

"Decapitation" is an archaic word, not to be pronounced in public. The media, reluctant to use the word, tended to skip over it. Just as the images of this kind of horrendous act were not broadcast, so the word itself became taboo. ISIS had... "slain" an American journalist. But CNN broke the taboo when, on August 20, 2014, it broadcast the news of the video that showed the execution of James Foley.[31] In a scene that has remained etched onto our collective memory, a black-clad jihadist stands next to the kneeling Foley, who is wearing an orange prisoner's jumpsuit. In an impeccable British accent, and brandishing a large knife, the jihadist admonishes President Obama to stop the US airstrikes against ISIS in Iraq. The executioner, Mohammed Emwazi, whose face is covered in the video, was known by the name of Jihadi John; he was killed in a Predator drone attack in 2015, on the outskirts of Raqqa, Syria; even *Dabiq*, the official online magazine of ISIS, reported his killing.

One need not see the video in its entirety, circumventing the censors and exposing oneself to surveillance from intelligence agencies, to be struck by the ostentatious cruelty of an execution that some have labeled as "porno-politics."[32] Upon close consideration, the ritual of decapitation, which reemerged after the September 11 attacks, already had a history spanning more than a decade. The first victim was the Israeli American journalist Daniel Pearl, kidnapped on January 23, 2002 and decapitated after nine days. Then the American Nick Berg was decapitated in 2004. The videos, as is well known, were suppressed, but their ghosts continue to haunt the Internet.

What is most offensive about these archaic scenes uploaded to the Web is not only the act of decapitation, but its ritual, cloaked in sacredness as it is. The severed head, which in Greek mythology was the symbol of the Medusa, so disgusting that it could turn into stone those who looked at it, is a *memento mori*. For an instant, the viewer sees her own death in that head with its rolling, lifeless eyes and face distorted in agony. Thus the severed head is both a trophy and a threat. The guillotine, inaugurated on April 25, 1792 in the Place de Grève in Paris, mechanized the act of execution, replacing manual torture with a more advanced technology. At the beginning of the modern age, when decapitation was the most common form of capital punishment, the executioner was considered to be an artist in the use of the sword, the axe, or the cleaver—even if he rarely succeeded in carrying out the beheading cleanly, in a single blow, which could have aroused the crowd's anger. But in general the executioner, that executive arm of power, was surrounded by an aura of sacred horror.

The ISIS executioners cut off their victim's head with a knife, following a ritual that is even older than that of the guillotine, but with symbolic references to that coldly rational form of decapitation. The jihadist puts on the garb of an executioner to play the part of the one who carries out the human sacrifice. His figure stands out against the backdrop of the sky and the desert, imposing in his theological–political role, because he is exercising military power following a liturgy of sacrifice. As if he were officiating at a religious ceremony, he reminds the modern citizen of the hidden presence of sacred sovereignty, which remains in an obscure background that is not penetrated by the power of the people. He is a reminder to the modern citizen that there, where sovereignty has never severed its tie with sacrifice, the mechanism of terror could decide to eliminate him—but just eliminate him, not sacrifice him, given that behind the façade of the citizen there is the *homo sacer*. He can only be killed, not sacrificed. The terrorist sees his victim as the reverse image of himself: if he himself can be sacrificed but not killed, then his victim, on the contrary, can be killed, but not sacrificed.

Sacred sovereignty is the sovereignty of God, which secularized modernity has attempted to do away with. Thus serial sacrifices are a response to a world that, even before it proclaimed that "God is dead," had decapitated God's sovereignty, leaving a disquieting void in democracy. And the jihadist comes on stage to challenge the atheists who have sought to decapitate the divine order. Those enlightened bourgeois who wanted to cut off the head of the sovereign will now have to be careful of losing their own heads. And this challenge has a philosophical dimension. The cold, systematic executions of the jihadists recall the French Revolution, but above all the culture of the Enlightenment, which sought to circumscribe everything, including religion, "within the limits of simple reason." The attack is against the head of modernity, which dreamt that it could make reason sovereign. But in refuting religion, modernity has prostrated itself before the idols of progress, money, and technology. In his bloody, dramatic way, mimicking divine violence in order to carry out a mythical violence, the jihadist hurls his provocation at the world, bringing out the theme of decapitated sovereignty.

# 10   Vulnerability, or innocence lost

It is not only the lack of a homeland that characterizes existence in the complex age of globalization. For years now, philosophers have been talking about vulnerability to indicate that, in addition to no longer feeling at home in the now open world, one is exposed to a *vulnus*, a wound that can be inflicted for no reason, harm that comes unexpectedly. After Levinas, who in recalling the exterminations of the twentieth century raised vulnerability to a philosophical category, while still calling upon the responsibility required by the absence of protection, the theme was taken up by Judith Butler, who in the wake of the September 11 attacks examined what life is like in a world pervaded by unprecedented aggression.[33] What is disconcerting is in fact the return of an age-old horror, of a violence that should not have a place in the civilized world, a violence that strikes the unarmed. Adriana Cavarero has rightly pointed out the difference between "unarmed," meaning those who cannot defend themselves because they are temporarily without weapons, and "vulnerable," which instead indicates the condition to which everyone now seems to be destined.[34]

The death of unarmed people in terrorist attacks such as the ones that took place in 2016 on the Promenade des Anglais in Nice on Bastille Day, or at a Christmas market in Berlin, forces us to think about a kind of violence that does not discriminate and that—as some have observed—seems to have inherited "genocidal" characteristics, in the sense that the executioners kill their victims for what they are, not for what they do.[35] According to this perspective, global terror has deterritorialized genocide. But this is true only in part, given that the term "genocide" is not totally appropriate because, in the terrorist attacks perpetrated by ISIS, *genos*— race or breed—is not distinguished. Rather it is a case of an omnicidal terrorism that, beyond their social class, race, religious faith, and ultimately even beyond their way of life, denies its victims the right to exist simply because of the place where they happen to be at that moment designated for apocalyptic purification.

Guilty of nothing except the place where their bodies happen to be, the unarmed, who reveal all their naked vulnerability, are the innocent who die anonymously, thrown into a pile of twisted limbs, unrecognizable shreds of flesh. The massacre is a disorganic totality that, however, reproduces the inhuman order of which the victims were a part—that indissoluble whole of which each person is a small node in a tightly woven net. This kind of attack wreaks "collateral damage" that is not dissimilar to what is caused by a drone.

Globalization means living in a society with unlimited responsibility, or rather unlimited irresponsibility, depending upon the way—trusting and exhortative, or cynical and resigned—in which the phenomenon is viewed. Pure innocence is lost. Because of the fragmentation of responsibility, everyone is always semi-innocent and semi-guilty at the same time. It is possible that, through an uninterrupted series of causes, a small advantage for one person will result in agony for someone somewhere else. It is even possible to be responsible for the death of others unknowingly, and yet be guilty.

The violence of hot blood that erupts in the city streets and squares has transformed western metropolises into cities of refuge. But nothing can protect against the "avenger of blood," the Go'el HaDahm, as he is called in Hebrew—that biblical figure that has become so contemporary, a figure that comes from the immense hinterland of desolation to roam the earth in the guise of a spirit of revolt, the rage of a people, or simple delinquency, before putting on the dismal mask of terror.

# 11   The negated ethics of the hostage

"I didn't look back, I didn't want to stare death in the face and I was sure I was going to die." These are the words of

Sigolène Vinson, the journalist who survived the *Charlie Hebdo* massacre in Paris on January 7, 2015.[36] A shout of "Allahu Akbar!" was followed by round after round of uninterrupted gunfire. After the screams of horror and the groans of suffering, and the death rattle of the first victim, a deathly silence fell. The air was pervaded by the smell of gunpowder. Vinson sought refuge behind a partition, beside the bleeding bodies of her friends. But the footsteps approached inexorably. One of the attackers ordered her to kneel down, aiming his Kalashnikov at her. He was dressed entirely in black and had a hood covering his face. "I looked at him. He had big dark eyes, a gentle look," recalls Vinson. The man in front of her, ready to kill her, was Saïd Kouachi. At first he seemed sure of himself. But she did not lower her eyes. She looked at him without hatred, without fear, and saw his expression change. Then Saïd Kouachi said: "Don't be afraid, calm down. I won't kill you. You're a woman, we don't kill women." And yet Elsa Cayat, a psychiatrist who was a columnist for the magazine, had been killed with an assault rifle a few seconds before, by Saïd's brother Chérif.

The carnage was interrupted when Vinson's and Kouachi's eyes unexpectedly met. The violence stopped. The terrorist revealed a glimpse of human weakness behind the steely mask of terror, while the unarmed victim almost unknowingly discovered that she had a powerful weapon—her own eyes. At that moment, Saïd Kouachi, a "negative hero" destined to insignificance, doomed to be a passing shadow that leaves no trace in the implacable indifference of others, found recognition, as tragic as it might be. Someone actually looked at him, considering him not a nothing, but rather an other, not to be ignored, not to be disregarded, in a sort of reverse asymmetry with eyes that looked up at him, questioning, supplicating. Someone else's life was in his hands. Perhaps he hadn't even wanted to have this power—a power that was almost not human anymore—a divine, or rather a demoniacal power. The recognition of that look, in which Saïd finally saw the value of his own life, stopped his gesture of death. Perhaps in his whole brief, futile existence, that was his only victory, his only wretched triumph.

Then Saïd Kouachi, along with his brother Chérif, headed headlong into violence again, sowing more terror and death.

After barricading themselves for hours inside a small printing firm in an industrial park in Dammartin-en-Goëlis on the northern outskirts of Paris, they were killed by French special forces at about 5:00 p.m. on January 9. This happened in a little less than ten minutes—while the two brothers fired the remaining ammunition in their Kalashnikovs. The outcome of the police operation was greeted as a success by the public. It is still not clear whether execution was chosen over arrest, as if a court trail were forbidden for those two young French terrorists, criminals who were so inhuman as to be judged unworthy of any redemption. And yet even the Nazis were granted a trial in Nuremberg. This leads one to believe that there is an unspoken rule that it is always and everywhere preferable to eliminate terrorists rather than put them on trial. The execution of Saïd and Cherif Kouachi was accepted as an inevitable fact, while the whole world, with the words summarized by the hashtag #jesuischarlie, was moved to defend freedom of the press and democracy.

Orphans who were made wards of the state at a young age, born in Paris of Algerian parents, Saïd and Chérif Kouachi seemingly divided up the roles they would play in life: Saïd did not drink or smoke, wasn't a womanizer, and had a certain charisma; turbulent and animated, his brother Chérif loved soccer and rap music and didn't hesitate to use his fists. They were bound together in an almost symbiotic relationship.[37] It wasn't inevitable that they would take the path of jihadism. Chérif frequented the mosque in the rue Tanger, where he met the preacher Farid Benyettou, who recruited fighters for al-Qaeda. In a piece published by the newspaper *Le Parisien*, Chérif told the story of the stages of his apprenticeship for going to Iraq to fight the American forces there: "Farid spoke to us about the advantages of suicide attacks. Thanks to him, my doubts disappeared [...] Farid provided a justification for my future death."[38] But shortly before Chérif was due to depart for Iraq, a message was intercepted by French security forces, and he was incarcerated in the Fleury-Mérogis maximum-security prison. When he was released after eighteen months of detention, he was not the same. During that period he met Amedy Coulibaly and Djamel Beghal; the latter is considered to be one of the masterminds of Islamist terrorism. Although he was under surveillance by antiterrorist agencies, in 2011 Chérif left for Yemen, where he was later joined by his brother Saïd. In 2014 both of their cell phones were put under surveillance, but seven months before the *Charlie Hebdo* massacre their phones stopped being surveilled, because it was believed that they were not involved in any terrorist activities. This was, in short, the story of the two Kouachi brothers, marked by petty crime, friendships with the wrong people, and prison—which paradoxically opened up a new horizon of meaning, until the culmination: death, inflicted on others and on themselves, in the name of a futile martyrdom. A name and two faces that reflected the "negative hero."

What happened during the *Charlie Hebdo* massacre, when Saïd Kouachi's Kalashnikov was stopped by the look in Sigolène Vinson's eyes, merits further reflection. Why take hostages, if any exchange is impossible, if there is no possibility of negotiation? Beyond the fatal strategy indicated by Baudrillard, beyond that homicidal challenge that paralyzes the system, emerges the figure of the hostage, which remains enigmatic. Perhaps the violent act with which a terrorist takes a hostage has a meaning, as recondite and unconfessed as it might be—a meaning that one might dare to define as ethical. And if, for that matter, ethics is also a way of seeing, it becomes understandable how a look could have been decisive.

A suggestion comes from Levinas, who elevated the word "hostage"—along with "obsession," "trauma," "substitution," and so on—to a hyperbole that articulates the constitutive passivity of the subject. Not at all disturbed by memories, nor disquieted by remorse, the modern subject has basked in the marvel of western freedom, advancing the secular claim of being legislator of the universe, a sovereign preoccupied only with his own sovereignty, disarmed only when confronted by death. In his prideful priority, in his illusory autonomy, in his emphatic identity, this detestable subject, always victorious over the differences of others, believed he could impose himself as an absolute subject, released from and unhampered by any responsibility—as if being responsible were an accidental attribute that the subject could choose not to assume, while continuing to exist. Levinas reversed the terms: for him, responsibility was not a supplement, but rather the constitutive node of every existence. This is why he related the subject, so full of himself, so imperialistically egocentric, to his extreme passivity, to his always being already offered to the other, consigned to the hands of others. "A subject is a hostage."[39] Responsibility toward others precedes the subject's possibility of being. Without the other, the subject would not even exist. Before me there is always the other who convokes me, interrogates me, to whom I am called upon to respond. There is no possibility of choice—because it is in the torsion toward the other, in that turning, that the subject is constituted. Responsibility takes precedence over freedom; it is an anarchical responsibility without principles and without an order, marked by that Hebrew *hinneni*, "here I am," with which in the Torah the subject is announced, responding to everything and for everyone—because the subject is a hostage through and through, "older than the ego," before principles. "It is through the condition of being hostage that there can be in the world pity, compassion, pardon and proximity."[40]

To be a hostage does not represent a borderline case; rather it is the irrecusable condition of everyone, who as a subject has to bear the burden of responsibility; the subject bears the weight even of that which is apparently indifferent to him or her, of that which has nothing to do with him or her. The ego is always in question—all the more so when it encounters the look of the other, the infiniteness of the other's face that, in its nakedness, from the depths of its defenseless eyes, paralyzes the subject's power, stops it, invoking the words in which every obligation is summed up: "Thou shalt not kill."[41]

In the inebriation of disinterest, one is tempted to escape the weight of that responsibility. Why me? Without thinking that this onus is the supreme human dignity. As if I were interchangeable, replaceable, as if I were confirming my own superfluity. In the cruelty of the terrorist act is concealed, undeciphered and undivulged, this message: "I am taking you hostage because you didn't care about me, because you didn't take me in when I was homeless, because, leaving me in my superfluous insignificance, you went beyond me in your sovereign indifference." The taking of a hostage is the violent deposition of the sovereign ego. It is the enraged gesture with which the ego is again consigned to the guilt that it had wanted to elude, to the expiation that it wanted to avoid. It is the rejection of a rejection, a "no," extreme and apocalyptic, to one who has rejected the unrejectable.

A wretched satisfaction that lasts only a few moments, in which the attacker seeks revenge for a whole life, a recognition of his existence that he has always longed for, a recognition of his significance for others, which is exhausted in that position of power, the rifle pointed at the head of the hostage. This position is not limited to deposing the sovereign ego; rather it seeks the same sovereignty for itself, in a reversal that has nothing revolutionary about it but that instead reiterates the same rejection—until, at the moment in which he exercises the absolute sovereignty over life or death, the face of the other is revealed to him, imploring him, recognizing the state of being a hostage, and he puts his rifle down.

# 12   The future in the time of terror

Only a few years ago, the present was full of hope for a "better future." But the shared hopes that united people and strengthened community ties began to fade away. Whether it is the unleashing of a planetary conflict, ecological disaster, financial crisis, the immigration that has become a phenomenon of our epoch, but also the precariousness that grips life today, or the violence that, in the most devious ways, manifests itself beyond the fragile confines of private life, the future now seems to be closing in on an imminent catastrophe. But it is terror that has marked an epochal turning point, forever changing our relationship with the time that is to come. One doesn't have to be clairvoyant to detect what would otherwise be inscrutable. Waiting for the next terrorist attack, we are overwhelmed by the certainty that the worst is yet to come.

If the future stands out threateningly against the polluted sky, the present is nothing more than the citadel of remaining privileges and the last satisfaction before everything collapses. So it seems as if it would be better if nothing changed. Instead of the unconditional "yes!" to what is to come, what prevails is a weak yet obstinate "no" in which is condensed the only secret hope that remains: the repetition of the same thing, the seductive, macabre dance of eternal return. But, as Nietzsche's *Zarathustra* shows, here expectation gives way to anguished, tragic memories of the past, while in that nostalgia there is a lessening of the attachment to existence here and now, which should incessantly project itself forward. The terror of the future strikes existence in its very essence.

The gravity of this unprecedented relationship with time is manifested in the current mania for analysis and predictions, in the frenzy to control time, in the disquietude of trying to control the future. But this flight into calculations can barely conceal the paralysis of a waiting that is full of apprehension, overflowing with anxiety. The unexpected exhibits its negative charge, the unforeseeable shows its most grim, imposing hostility. The time to come, which always has a tomorrow, is circumscribed in a diffident future, entrenched in the immediacy of the present, fixed on the unpresentable of which all the signs are harbingers, a time with no tomorrow that resembles a future anterior. And on this horizon, where diffidence, fear, and rage leave their mark on relationships, the other does not emerge with the fruitful transport of otherness, but rather looms with the asphyxiating obsession of terror.

But is this effect perhaps intentional? Terror is able to dominate precisely because it looks toward the future. The future of terrorism resides in fear of the future. If it looms and dominates with its intimidation, it is because it uses a weapon—the most terrifying weapon—that both comes from the future and is aimed toward the future.

Attacks are imminent; danger always lies in ambush. The anonymous invisibility of the enemy, the indeterminateness of his or her cause, the difficulty in localizing aggression that could be unleashed anywhere make the threat all the more indecipherable and disturbing. The wound cannot heal because it is not circumscribed by the past; if it were, it would only be necessary to process the trauma, and then turn the page. But terror, as Derrida observed, "wounds and leaves forever open an unconscious scar [...] this weapon is terrifying because it comes from the *to-come*, from the *future*."[42] What has already happened will happen again, with the same cruel unpredictability. It will happen again.

The physics of terror, as it is postponed in the unpredict-able randomness of the future, acts strategically, striking even potential victims. Thus terror keeps everyone on the alert, under the gun, but also envisions a perpetual adaptation. The future becomes a time of violence that expands to include everyday life. Beyond the single living creature, life itself is irremediably damaged and wounded in this new chapter in the history of human destruction.

# 4

# The New Phobocracy

In our neighborhoods and in our suburbs, there is no longer the effigy of Che Guevara, but of Bin Laden.[1]

The Vanguard of Terror has become modernity's opposition—vicious, spectacular, and effective all at once—that speaks certain truths to the modern in a manner that no language of Reason dares to.[2]

## 1  Clash of civilizations, class struggle, or "holy" war?

There are three prevailing paradigms in the current interpretation of terrorism: the "clash of civilizations," according to the influential formula of Samuel Huntington; class struggle and, more generally, the idea that what feeds violence is great economic inequalities; and, finally, the notion of a "holy" war waged in the name of religion. While all three of these paradigms have some correct insights and fruitful elements, they are nevertheless inadequate; they offer a simplified, at times dangerously reductive vision of a very complex phenomenon.

Terrorism is closely connected to globalization, of which it is not only an effect, but also in a certain way the driving force. If on the one hand terrorism proclaims its "no" to the notion of a unified planet, on the other hand it ignores all national frontiers, cancels out boundaries, annuls differences—between war and peace, between military and civilian, between a state of emergency and a state of normalcy. The terrorist is an agent of hybridization. The gory scene of a car bombing is strongly symbolic: by sending the "martyr" up in flames it tears apart both the body of the terrorist and the bodies of others; it causes a commingling of blood and bodies to the point of impeding identification. It confuses, dissimulates, camouflages identities.

This explains why it is difficult to define once and for all what a "terrorist" is, unless one falls back on one of the numerous shortcuts that portray this figure as a bloodthirsty monster or a psychopath. There are other interpretations, always partial and approximate: terrorists are victims of economic crisis, living proof of the failure of integration, new incarnations of Herostratus in search of fame, children of the Internet and video games, products of a society dominated by sensationalism. The list could go on and on.

In delineating the "clash of civilizations," Huntington perhaps had the sole merit, as Arjun Appadurai has pointed out, of having grasped early on the feeling of enmity toward the West that was spreading throughout the Islamic world.[3] But Huntington's monolithic, fixed idea of "civilization," from which history seems to be excluded, is fundamentally unacceptable—as if the West—to confine ourselves to philosophy—were not indebted to the Islam of Aristotle's commentators, and as if Islamic mysticism were imaginable without Plato. In the globalized world, the image of two monolithic blocs circumscribed by criteria of race, territory, and religion appears to be not only mistaken, but also harmful. The immediate and best-known effect of this perspective is to condemn the entire variegated Muslim world, accusing it of being archaic and antiprogressive.

Rather than speaking of a "clash of civilizations," we should speak of a civilization of clashes all around the world that produces outbreaks that are akin to a low-level war. Contributing to this in a determining way is the unbridled power of global capitalism, which, favoring a small group of winners, leaves in its wake masses of losers who are not only excluded from any possibility of emancipation, but also profoundly humiliated. And yet privation, poverty, and unemployment are not direct causes of terrorism—they are not what triggers that extreme choice, nor are they what could clarify it. Nor can social justice, once the banner of fighting organizations, be seen to be explicitly the cause. The poor are the first victims of terrorism. And it is not only the ambiguous role played by countries like Saudi Arabia or Kuwait that casts the shadow of other interests.[4] The question is much more complicated when we take into consideration the disturbing convergence between streams of financial capital and of transnational terrorism that, thanks to a common network structure, come close to complicity. Suffice it to think of the immense arms trade.

No less reductive is the third paradigm, which interprets terrorism as a synonym of fundamentalism; this is an unjustified semantic drift that causes further serious misunderstandings. One can be a fundamentalist, radical, or radicalized without being a "terrorist." The step from here to blaming Islam is a short one. Islamophobia becomes very handy. But if Islam is targeted, why not Christianity and Judaism? The front becomes broader. The notion of a clash of civilizations is dusted off, and in a new version it is presented as the clash between enlightened, progressive laicism and religion—which, having reemerged into the public sphere, would purportedly be ready, in all its traditions, for a new theocratic exterminism.

"Religion is war" is the cry of a primordial stereotype that has never disappeared.[5] From one monotheist religion to another, from one religious text to another all the way back to the Old Testament, where it is imagined that the proof of that "theology of terror can be found," religion is seen as the cause of all past, present, and future evils.

This paradigm, corroborated also by the notion of a "clash of monotheisms," seems to be most widespread now. If it cannot be denied that jihadist violence has a religious matrix, it is nevertheless unacceptable to equate Islam with terrorism or to criminalize monotheism. This is once again a drastic, schematic attempt to find an orientation in today's convulsed scenario—an attempt to find a clear front line, a definite frontier where in fact lines of conflict intersect, connect, and blend together.

## 2 The offensive of radicalized secularism

The idea of a clash between secular reason and "the sacred" reveals a profound sense of unease that can be attributed to the purported "return" of religion to the public sphere. Since the luminous progress of reason has not been achieved, the dry river is full of the sand of secularization, incapable of responding to the thorny questions of the new century. Those who believe in the "original sin" of religion can barely tolerate its return. Irritation is mixed with an exacerbated disillusionment. Secular reason becomes radicalized in a sort of laicism that can take on extreme forms.

The reasons should be sought in the global context. Secularization has always been connected to the nation-state and has been able to affirm itself in modernity, when politics, concealing its own religious foundations, has ended up sacralizing the state, becoming a sort of civic religion. The decline of the nation-state brings with it the crisis of a secularism that arose through a fictitious separation between church and state. It is not by chance that it is precisely the secular voices that have had a difficult time going beyond the confines of the nation-state, while paradoxically in the McWorld of today it has been religions that have played a leading role not only in private life, but in public life as well. It is impossible to ignore the role of religions on the international scene.

The clashes between religion and laicism in France and, more generally, in the European context have been provoked by the entrance of Islam onto the scene. While Judaism and Christianity, renouncing many prerogatives, made a sort of pact with the state in the early times of modernity, Islam has only recently begun to enter into the "secular pact." This has brought to light a difficulty that is related to other religions as well. In fact, Judaism and Christianity had to renounce their political dimension, without that renunciation ever having been definitive.

In this clash, which is still in progress, secularism has unleashed an attack not only against religions, but also against "monotheism." From this perspective, if "God is violence," then the cause should be sought in his oneness. Theses of this kind, which have spread more or less everywhere, have found legitimacy in the very controversial studies of the Egyptologist Jan Assmann, who has gone so far as to see in monotheism the theological–political paradigm of dictatorship.[6] According to this theory, where gods dominate, there is tolerance; where a single God reigns, there is violence. Re-proposed by Sloterdijk, this thesis has caused a rupture in the world of philosophy, where an opposite stance was taken by Derrida, who defended the three monotheistic religions, which he believed were called upon to engage in a dialogue that would be capable of orienting major political choices.[7]

For their part, the three monotheistic religions consider with a certain diffidence the aspiration of the "culture of secularism" to be a neutral meeting ground. The negative results are already there for everyone to see. Multiculturalism, in its self-proclaimed universality, is a sort of artificial language, without depth; it imposes abstract connections, ideas that are destined to remain aleatory. The grammar of reciprocity is not learned here, nor is the syntax of alterity. Multicultural secularism not only does not mediate between different religions, the de-culturation of which it in fact promotes; rather it makes more acute the clash between the religious and the secular fronts.

# 3   Hermeneutics counters violence

The "return" of religions to the public sphere has been accompanied by a singular phenomenon, which Olivier Roy calls "holy ignorance." In the era of globalization, rather than becoming smaller, the gap between culture and religion is becoming larger.

Secularism is not exempt from responsibility. If it is presumed that the Bible is a conglomeration of dogmas, a series of bloody episodes, then why read it? If religion is no more than blind faith, superstition, and dogma, what sense would there be in having knowledge of it? Judged from the apparent height of enlightened reason, religion is nothing more than a superfluous, harmful obstacle that should be removed with a peremptory gesture. But often, in this peremptoriness, the secularist reveals his or her own undeniable fanaticism.

Secularism brands religion as ignorant, reviving age-old stereotypes, re-proposing dangerous prejudices that have grown over the centuries. Paradoxically, the "culture of secularism," by stigmatizing religions as non-culture and by expelling them from the shared cultural patrimony, endorses, fosters, and in part promotes "holy ignorance." The repercussions are devastating.

The gap between culture and religion has been caused first and foremost by a rebirth of religion, which has appeared in the secularized public sphere clad in purity and with a militant character. In this way religion has appropriated the fanatical fundamentalist image that secularism had projected upon it. This is why it is ambiguous to speak of a "return" of religion. On the contrary—it is the most extreme, charismatic versions of religion (Salafism, evangelism, and so on) that have been successfully imposed in our time.[8] When separated from traditional culture, religions can more easily be presented as a new universal, capable of unifying the globalized world.

These versions of religion reduce the polyphonic character of tradition, from which they nevertheless derive, to the tune of a single truth. Where there is militancy there is no time for study, much less for the hermeneutics of written texts. For this kind of believer, God speaks without a context. Faith is enough. "Holy ignorance" puts up barriers between believers of different faiths, as well as between believers and non-believers. Every intermediate space is abolished; shared values and ideals that could foster dialogue are canceled out. The believer rises up as the one and only exponent of what is "holy," in contrast to a profane world that has expanded to include everyone who might otherwise seem to be a believer as believers in doubt, or non-practicing believers.

While this inflexibility can be found in all religions, nevertheless the religion that seems to have been affected most profoundly is Islam, which appears to be in the process of being torn apart from the inside. The front line traverses the space of the holy text and separates the exegetes from the doctrinaires. This is a clash between those who read sacred texts in order to interpret them and those who make those texts their own in order to turn them into an instrument of domination. The former take up the interpretations to which the Quran has given rise throughout history, while the latter turn the text of the Quran into stone, reducing it to a single, immutable code that they call upon in a purely and exceedingly legalistic spirit, in order to impose respect for sharia. It would be a mistake not to take into consideration, in all its gravity, this clash that is taking place within Islam. The Islamists, convinced that they are the only ones who are faithfully following the Quran, the only ones who possess the absolute truth, mistake the text of the Quran for a manual for carrying out jihad.

Resistance to terror takes place through reading. Terrorists of every ilk refuse to read. It is here that hermeneutics can reveal its potential for liberation. Violence does not reside in the "sacred text," but rather in the presumption that that text can be taken literally—for example, the Torah as *verbum mysticum*. It is not by chance that a decisive role in the Jewish tradition is played by the Talmud, the reading of which runs through the centuries in an open dialogue— because reading does not mean idolizing a text, but rather opening it up to its multiple meanings, unfolding it in the infinite ways in which it can be interpreted.

For that matter, "religion" in the etymological sense refers both to the action of reading and to a community's connection to tradition. Those who read sacred texts are open to others, with whom they can see affinities and differences. Where the hermeneutics of texts is not practiced, one remains mute before the ostentation of a purported "truth," which should instead be immediately deconstructed.

# 4   Sedative or stimulant?
## Religion according to Marx

Terrorists are often labeled as fanatics. In this accusation are condensed all the disgust and all the blame that pervade the West of the third millennium when faced with the mind-boggling phenomenon of a religion that has grown to be a political power. An aberration! Doesn't religion belong to the past? It doesn't even make sense to talk about it. Seen from this perspective, this calling upon God is nothing more than a flimsy pretext, a remnant of ignorance, a hiccup of history, the symptom of social unease, an optical illusion that covers up economic relationships. And anyway, didn't Marx already resolve the problem by pointing out that religion is "the opium of the people"?

A veritable topos of the Marxist vulgate, this formula is so well known that any questioning of it seems to be unjustified. According to the author of *Das Kapital*, religious superstition is the drug that numbs the minds of workers, leading them to accept the exploitation of which they are the victims. If this sickness—the domination of the middle class—were to be eliminated, then the false remedy—the recourse to the opium of religion—would become superfluous.

Given that Marx's texts are not known today as well as they once were, we should go back to the passage from which the famous formula was taken. Attentive to the Jewish tradition from which Marx came, Michael Löwy has indicated several precedents for that image. Heinrich Heine in 1840 and Moses Hess in 1843 had already introduced the opium metaphor to emphasize the narcotic power of religion, which can make bearable the unhappy awareness of being enslaved.[9] The young Marx took up this metaphor in his *Critique of Hegel's "Philosophy of Right,"* published in 1844. He wrote:

> The wretchedness of religion is at once an expression of and a protest against real wretchedness. Religion is the sign of the oppressed creature, the heart of a heartless world and the soul of soulless conditions. It is the opium of the people.[10]

At the time he wrote this, Marx was not yet a Marxist. He was a leftist Hegelian who, distancing himself from the Enlightenment, did not see religion as a conspiracy of the clergy. Rather, in the wake of Feuerbach, he considered religion to be a complex form of alienation, which he interpreted in an ahistorical way, without considering it in the light of the class struggle.

Alienation in this sense means that human beings project their own capacities onto heaven, thus becoming estranged from themselves. Marx took a further step when, in *The German Ideology*, which he wrote with Engels in 1846, he saw in religion a spiritual production, a set of ideas and representations—in short, an ideology against which it was necessary to rebel, so that the creators would cease to bow before their own creations. It was useless to follow false chimeras into the sky—it was existence on earth that needed to be changed. Looking down, there emerged with all its hardships the condition of the workers who, under the domination of capitalism, no longer recognized themselves in the merchandise that they produced. And this was alienation in its most naked, pitiless, inhuman, and disturbing form: economic alienation. Merchandise became fetishes that acquired an autonomous power, a sacred force over the workers. The criticism of the "fetishism of commodities" that Marx outlined in *Das Kapital* sprang from religion.[11] This attests to the decisive role played by the religious model. God is there, capital is here: but in the end, in both cases, the individual is despoiled for the profit of an alien power.

According to Marx, religious alienation and economic exploitation follow an analogous process. But there is an unresolved relationship of tension between them. Religious alienation is the mother of all alienations, the form par excellence of being separate. The gesture with which a supplicant's arms are raised to the heavens is already a sign of schism; supplicants are separated from themselves, not reconciled. Marx believed that religious alienation would vanish when the secular foundation for it—economic exploitation—would be gone. For him, there was no other way to think about emancipation. This is why he believed that criticism of theology should give way to criticism of political economy.

Marx believed that the day would come when the proletariat—the class of slaves, deprived of any law of their own, a universal class capable of dragging all of humanity along with it—would awaken to a new world where there would no longer be private property, or production of commodities, or exploitation. At that moment the opium would evaporate; the subterfuges that surround the products of labor would go away; the phantom mist of religion would disappear.

But the day was slow in coming. Capitalism did not give way. The working class met with one defeat after another. When Paris was drowning in a blood bath in 1871, Marx fell into a deep depression; for a certain period he stopped writing.

The spirit of religion did not disappear. Indeed, it returned, under the oppressive sky of capital, to denounce the fact that alienation still undermined human existence, to warn that emancipation had not been achieved. Poverty was there; religion remained as a sign of that. Its spirit was the specter that haunted Marx; it was the ghost that obsessed the father of communism. And his descendants would not become free of that specter. Convinced that he was the only one capable of dissipating the chimeras of spirituality, Marx instead failed to exorcise his own demons. *Specters of Marx*—this is the title of a famous series of lectures by Derrida. How could one not think of the famous opening lines of the *Communist Manifesto*? "A specter is haunting Europe—the specter of communism." The reference is to the *Gespenst* [ghost], the new specter that was terrorizing the ruling classes on the old continent. But Derrida also recognized in the specter the most important rhetorical or polemical figure to which Marx had recourse.[12] Seen from this perspective, Marx's work reveals itself to be a gigantic phantomachia, and Marx himself an indefatigable hunter of ghosts—the ghost of religion first and foremost. Of course, Marx did not believe in religion, and yet he thought of nothing else. Without having exorcised religion, he left the specter of religion as an inheritance to those who came after him. From that time on, religion has obsessed and disturbed the left, which has clumsily attempted to hide it to a great degree. The return of that specter, in more or less fundamentalist garb, caught the left unprepared.

Religion was the big question for Marx. This was strongly stressed by Jean-Yves Calvez in a chapter on politics and religion in his book *Marx et le marxisme*.[13] Although in his private life Marx had no difficulty ridding himself of religion, this grandson of a rabbi never underestimated the power of dissent and revolt that religion maintains; so he never lost sight of the connection between theology and politics. Religion played a leading role not only in Marx's imagination, but also in his theoretical project and in his political promise. It left its mark on the spirit of Marxism in its revolutionary aspirations.

Sedative or stimulant? The double character of religion surfaces when Marx says, in an almost contradictory way, that religion is an expression of wretchedness but also of protest. It can lead those who are enslaved to resignation, but it can also call them to insurrection. Marx had certainly not forgotten the Exodus.

After Marx, the left was divided between the Enlightenment view, which, taking only the opium image as valid, condemned religion as a reactionary tool, and the utopian view, which detected in religion the clandestine, messianic river of subversion. There are innumerable examples. In the German Peasants' War of 1525 led by Thomas Münzer, the peasants were demanding that the Realm of God be instated on earth, which is—as Engels observed—an anticipation of communism. And while Rosa Luxembourg maintained that there was a connection between the workers' movement and ancient Judeo-Christian messianism, Ernst Bloch saw religion as the most significant form of utopianism, in which the principle of hope was preserved.

# 5   The left and jihad

In its internationalist ideal, in its cosmopolitan tradition, the left—the avant-garde of insurgents—could not help but align itself with the "damned of the earth" from the time of the earliest anticolonial struggles. For decades, the great socialist fleet crossed the oceans, following the star of emancipation. It navigated currents and eddies, in the certainty of dominating the flow of history.[14]

Religion, the rival sister of revolution, has not been an insuperable cliff. In fact the opposite has happened. In Latin America in the 1960s, the atheistic left found a formidable ally in the Christian movement known as "liberation theology," which combined the gospels and the class struggle, the ancient prophets and the new spirit of revolt. From El Salvador to Chile, the priests of the slums, often at the cost of their own lives, made themselves the spokespeople of the poor; demanding justice and equality, they called upon the people to rise up against military dictatorships and imperialism. The left could not help but realize that this was a shared struggle.

"Liberation theology" thus constituted a precedent that is still not the subject of a great deal of reflection. If the left could form an alliance with that militant form of Christianity, why couldn't the same thing be repeated with Islam? This question, which not by chance has remained open for the Latin American left, which is geopolitically distant from global terror, neglects the difference between Christianity and Islam. This is in keeping with a basic indifference that the left has shown toward "religion," even though the specter of religion has haunted it from the beginning.

When Islamism became a force on the international scene, the left tried to find affinities. Militants from both the left and Islamism sought to unmask the hypocrisy of western democracies and to end the iniquity of the market. But the Algerian War of Independence already represented an early disillusionment. In a short time the capital, Algiers, was chosen as a privileged place for world rebellion, in which leaders from the Afroamerican movements, European intellectuals, Vietnamese rebels, and Latin American guerrillas came together, and where, in 1965, Che Guevara gave his famous speech against imperialism. Nevertheless, it soon became clear that, for the Algerian leaders of the National Liberation Front, religion was not a veil that one day could be torn away to reveal the class struggle behind it; rather, it was the beating heart of the revolution.

The Iranian Revolution of 1979 marked a definitive rupture. Islam was fast becoming a protagonist of contemporary history, making its own mark on political theology, which had been obviated by the western left. In Khomeini's Iran, those who would soon be called "Islamists," rather than collaborating with the progressive forces, seemed to want to marginalize or even replace them. In spite of this, the left was tempted to look upon that revolution, as far from the left as it may have been, with a certain sympathy; it was still believed that it could make the yeast of emancipation rise. If the oppressed were fighting, the left should be by their side.

Between October 1978 and February 1979, Michel Foucault was in Tehran as a correspondent for the Italian newspaper *Corriere della Sera*. At first Foucault was enthusiastic about that revolution, which he was eager to watch unfolding. He interviewed workers and students: "What do you want?" He was expecting them to answer "Revolution," but instead their reply was: "An Islamic government." Foucault recognized a strong "political spirituality" and had to admit that religion was not the veil that disguised the revolution, but rather its true face. "Islam—which is not simply a religion, but a way of life, belonging to a history and a civilization—risks becoming a gigantic powder keg," he wrote in an article in the *Corriere della Sera* dated February 11, 1979.[15]

But Foucault was a lone voice, and those articles, in which he already detected in revolutionary Islamism an unthought-of alternative to the West, were neglected for a long time. Žižek has been one of the few to return to Foucault's articles about Iran, and indeed to call for the abandonment of an old left-wing taboo: the ban on any criticism of Islam, which had been branded as Islamophobia.[16]

For decades, a fatal ambivalence dominated the questionings and the choices of the left. Was Islam a possible ally, or an adversary to be feared? A necessary accomplice, or an imponderable rival?

At the end of the 1970s, in spite of obstacles, adversities, and defeats, there still shone the light of hope, showing a glimmer of the story's tomorrow, when the oppressed would finally be liberated. The setbacks were no more than hidden tunnels dug here and there by that good old mole of the revolution.

Caught between a capitalism that was anything but defeated and a Stalinism that suffocated any freedom, the western left, already as early as the Cold War, had taken the path toward the third world, where it was hoped that an increasingly solid alliance could be forged with the oppressed of the earth. But, upon close consideration, that impulse was too late in coming. For some time, capitalism—thanks also to technology—had gone beyond borders, spreading on a planetary scale, exploiting, colonizing, raising profit to the status of a universal law.

After the fall of the Berlin Wall, the political landscape changed. The arrogance of the market sealed the victory of economic liberalism—a victory that some were in a hurry to declare definitive, as if the history of the world should conclude with that insolent triumph. For the left, in all its variants, the disappointments multiplied. And yet, at the end of the old century and the dawn of the new century, third-worldism, heir to the struggles for liberation and to the internationalist commitment, took on different and more vast contours. From Seattle to Bangkok, from Porto Alegre to Paris, a non-global galaxy was forming—a galaxy that included non-governmental organizations, unions, ecological associations, and political groups that were fighting for the rights of those who had no rights. It was believed that another way of life was possible, under the banner of solidarity and sharing. Alternative lifestyles were tried out and, moving from the world of forgotten peripheries, there was hope of "another world," beyond the eternal return of the market. "Other-worldism" was spoken about like a new International, united around the need to combat the McWorld in which techno-liberal globalization was taking place. The idea was that the condition of the world should be rejected and a world without nation-states should be envisaged. But, lacking a clear political project, the revolution without frontiers became a mobilization with no tomorrow.

In was at this juncture that Islamism burst spectacularly on the scene of history. With its transnational logic, it destroyed the old grammar of national boundaries and threatened sovereign territories; with its transcendent aspirations, it hurled a challenge at the profane immanence of capitalism.

But the threat also loomed over the left, which was in danger of being ousted from its role as the atavistic adversary of capitalism. What was to be done now with the third world? The decision was complicated and arduous. Should the leftists distance themselves from the Islamist movements, to stand with women and homosexuals, to defend civil rights and freedom of expression, ending up coalescing with the liberal currents? Or should they chose to have a socialist–Islamist "united front," in the name of the shared anti-imperialist struggle? The difficulties with which the left struggled should be read as intrinsic contradictions of Islam. If the left wanted to avoid making rash judgments about a movement that was not a reactionary monolith, then it needed to take a "wait and see" attitude and make a temporary alliance with the Islamists. This tactic was proposed in the pamphlet *The Prophet and the Proletariat* published in 1994 by the British activist Chris Harman. Without minimizing the shock caused by the advance of Islamism, Harman believed that he could recognize in that political program not so much the desire to return to the Islam of the seventh century as the will to change the world order. Thus he maintained that the state should not be supported against the Islamists, nor the Islamists against the state. But he maintained that, "[w]here the Islamists are in opposition, our rule should be, 'with the Islamists sometimes, with the state never.'"[17] The criterion for the choice to be made was the risky, slippery one of choosing who should be the main enemy. It was impossible to fight on more than one front. If imperialism—the main enemy—was to be defeated, it would be necessary to make an alliance with the secondary enemy, even if that were the Taliban. This explains the support that, at least until the Arab Spring, the third-world leftists gave to fundamentalist organizations like Hezbollah in Lebanon and Hamas in Gaza, arriving, in some demonstrations, even to the point of flying their own flags along with those of groups affiliated with the Muslim Brotherhood.

It is not difficult to detect, behind this tactic, the western arrogance of feeling capable of enlightening those who are still immersed in darkness—the paternalistic pretension of channeling the unhappiness of those younger brothers who follow the wave of religious integralism in order to recruit them to become part of the great socialist fleet. It was thought that, after having denounced the wretchedness of reality, religion would disappear, leaving the revolution to take over. It would be sufficient to leverage radical Islam in order to mobilize the oppressed masses of the Islamic world. Sooner or later, it was believed, the flames of that fundamentalism would spark a worldwide revolution, if only the left were there to encourage and guide it.

But the opposite happened. As the Lebanese Marxist Gilbert Achcar has written, "reactionary forces using Islam as an ideological banner prevailed in most Muslim-majority countries, fanning the flames of Islamic fundamentalism to incinerate the remnants of the left."[18] The optimism of the left was completely unfounded. Over the years, the power relationships have reversed. Without resolving its own contradictions or betraying its own roots, jihadism has shown an extraordinary capacity to profit from the new ultraliberal forms of capitalist globalization and high-tech communication, going so far as to become the leading player of the opposition to the West—an affront to the left. The left has had to admit that from the oppressed of the earth there has emerged an army of hackers ready to die so that centuries-old laws and customs may triumph. Thus, as the socialist fleet seems to have run aground, Marx's heirs have discovered that in recent years, following a very different compass, others have learned to navigate better than they have the boundary-less ocean of universal rage and hope.

# 6 Spanish brigades, Syrian brigades

In its fervor, jihadism seems to be the only ideal capable of mobilizing the masses in the four corners of the globe today, challenging the world order. Jihadists by the thousands are ready to face death, gathering, also virtually, beneath the black flag of ISIS that bears the profession of Islamic faith and flaunts the seal of the prophets, an explicit reference to the advent of the Mahdi, the redeemer who will appear before the end of the world. The geopolitical place of the final battle that will precede redemption is the land called Sham, from which comes the Arabic-language acronym DAESH (al-Dawla al-Islamiya fi al-Iraq wa al-Sham), the "Islamic State of Iraq and the Levant." The heart of the East that is rising up is in Syria, where, according to the prophecies, everything will be reconciled before the kingdom of God is proclaimed at the end of times. In the jihadist imagination, the Levant is the place where time will come to an end, where the fate of the world will be decided in a final, apocalyptic clash.

Jihadists come not only from the countries of the Maghreb and the Middle East, but also from western cities—Paris and Brussels, London and Milan, Stockholm and Frankfurt, Moscow and Sydney—from which they travel to outposts in Turkey and then cross the border toward Mosul and Aleppo. There are more than 20,000 of them from more than 80 countries—the "foreign fighters" who have joined the ranks of the jihadists.

These brigades of worldwide Jihadism recall a precedent that stands out indelibly against the backdrop of the history of the twentieth century, when in 1936 more than 30,000 volunteers belonging to the International Brigades joined the Spanish Republican Army in the fight against fascism and Nazism.

As troubling as this comparison might seem, there are in fact many affinities that justify it, beginning with the military commitment and the international solidarity of the fighters in both groups. The decisive push for both is the urgent need—reasoned or instinctive—to respond to a call to come to the aid of comrades exposed to the violence of Franco's army in the former case or of brothers dedicated to martyrdom in the latter. Existential motives and personal destinies join with common ideals, shared aspirations, universal visions. Similarly, hope and desperation, patience and anxiety, confidence and hesitancy, waiting and disquietude are mingled together. Indignation, which feeds the destructive impulse, cannot conceal the demand for justice.

Also similar is the fighters' sense of leave-taking, which has a definitive flavor. Whether on a train departing for the Pyrenees or an airplane leaving for Ankara, the fighters' break with their past life signals a voluntary farewell to their former existence—with no certainty of return. Individuals offer themselves as a sacrifice for a cause that is bigger than they are and in which they believe they can recognize the meaning of their own possible death.

But the affinities end here, and the differences are profound. Whether he was a socialist, an anarchist, or a Trotskyite, the volunteer in the International Brigades came from a working-class background and from a militant culture, and sometimes had military experience; he was a member of a political party or a union; his difficult choice had been the result of attending popular assemblies and public debates, mostly in open spaces, under the auspices of the Communist International and with the more or less explicit support of some governing authority.

By contrast, the jihadist, male or female (for there is a significant presence of women in the movement), is mobilized to a large degree by the Internet, in a spontaneous way, in the shadows, clandestinely, often in solitude, without the filter of a political party, and above all without any kind of political preparation.

But the differences have to do especially with the jihadist's relationship with history and with death. The members of the International Brigades were certain that the battle that awaited them in Spain would be decisive for the fate of humanity. Many were pacifists. They would have preferred to avoid that sacrifice; they ardently desired to live. They crossed the Pyrenees in the hope of accelerating history in order to make it more human.

The jihadists, instead, face death, which for them, far from being a sacrifice, is victory itself. Certain that the end of the world is looming, they don't want to accelerate history but to leave it behind. They are not thinking of permanent revolution, but rather—once politics has been abolished—of permanent redemption.

# 7   The terrorism of global capitalism

The overuse of certain terms can often be misleading. One example is the term "multiculturalism," which has led some to see the conflicts that are playing out on the world's stage as friction between a particular identity and a universal belonging. But, as Étienne Balibar has pointed out, the clash is between rival universalisms that are fundamentally incompatible.[19] To be even more explicit, one might speak of "dreams," following a suggestion of Sloterdijk. Alongside the capitalist dream and the communist dream, jihadism represents a third dream, an eastern alternative to communism.

A third complication has come to undermine the dogma of the "world market," but above all it demonstrates what readers of Walter Benjamin have known for a long time and is now coming clearly to light: the fact that capitalism has always been much more than a simple relationship of production. In the immanence of the power of acquisition, capitalism has absorbed, disposed, and organized not only labor but all of life. The two "dreams"—capitalism and jihadism—therefore have much in common. They are both political *as well as* religious. The emergence of radical Islam is more comprehensible, even in its most antagonistic form, if one also recognizes that, for some time now, capitalism has entered into a state of extreme political and religious radicalization. Its epochal triumph, sealed after the fall of the Berlin Wall, has been celebrated in a militant Fukuyamism, a vision in which the universal interests of humanity are

placed at the mercy of capital. With the "end of history,"
Fukuyama announced in 1992 that capitalism would never
be replaced.[20] This was a finalistic, theological, and in essence
also an apocalyptic announcement. The same can be said
of jihadism.

Jihadism and capitalism are not only ideologies; they are
also religions transformed into ways of life; conversely, they
are ways of life that are dictated by religious principles. The
mirror image of an intransigent puritanism that demands
obedience to a single passion, jihadism is the response of
ascetic passion to that singular, violent, narcissistic passion
in which the commandment of capitalism is summed up:
"Enjoy!"

Enjoy, savor, revel, profit ... under the conditions of capitalism, of course. This activistic care for one's own existence
is concentrated on enjoying the comforts that are publicized
in the media, but on the basis of a debt that can never be
paid, a sin that can never be forgiven. In a sibylline phrase,
Benjamin called capitalism "a pure religious cult, perhaps the
most extreme there ever was"—a cult that could count on a
"permanent duration." There is no truce, no pardon. The
sacred pomp of marketing, the ritual of earning money, the
ostentation of consumerism are unstoppable. Capitalism is a
cult that requires obsessive celebration. It would seem that it
is always a celebration—but it never really is. There is no
difference between day and night when time is always and
only measured in terms of money. If the cult is uninterrupted,
it is thanks to the apotheosis of debt. "Capitalism is the first
case of a blaming, rather than a repenting cult."[21] It could
not be otherwise for a religion that permits neither salvation
nor redemption. Beneath the heaven of capitalism there is
only "cosmic desperation."

Opposed to the cult of unhappy emancipation, to the
terror of a tragic, always the same existence disguised as progress, is jihadism, which seeks to impose expiation but instead
emerges in the form of expression and protest, without,
however, being able to guide a new uprising of the downtrod-
den or to channel energy against the prevailing system, even
though it is an image of the world. The spread of terrorism
produces a new, imponderable consumption of security, from
which global capitalism may be able to profit.

# 8   Democracy put to the test by antiterrorism

From the depths of his cell in the Guantánamo detention camp, where he underwent torture of every kind for more than ten years before being declared innocent and released, Mohamedou Ould Slahi wondered whether democracy had passed the test to which it had been subjected after September 11, 2001.[22]

It is not possible to give a definitive answer to this question. But it can be said that before that day neither Hitler nor Stalin nor anyone else had struck such a hard blow to western democracy, damaging its basic principles. Perhaps it is here that the secret objective of jihadism is hidden: the posthumous victory of Osama bin Laden was not the collapse of the Twin Towers, but rather the Patriot Act. As early as September 21, 2001, bin Laden had told a journalist: "I tell you, freedom and human rights in America are doomed. The US government will lead the American people, and the West in general, into an unbearable hell and a choking life."[23]

After the elimination of bin Laden and the dismantling of a good part of the Al-Qaeda network, which in 2011 was believed to have been defeated, terrorism continued to proliferate in Syria, Iraq, Libya, Yemen, Somalia, Nigeria, Mauritania, and Mali, spreading, in even more virulent forms, in the form of interposed groups and under new names and acronyms, from Jabhat al-Nusra to ISIS, while democratic institutions everywhere have been eroding, as have civil liberties. The "war on terror" has been revealed to be the self-destruction of democracy—to the point that, even in countries that are traditionally the most democratic, soon governments will dare to impose a non-democracy.

Terror and democracy are the two fruits of modernity. Democracy means not needing terror any more. As Hegel understood well, terror is the price that the modern human has to pay for learning that abstract freedom needs laws; it is a stage on the journey to the modern state—in fact it is an episode, painful and indispensable, in the maturation of humanity. In this sense, democracy is always post-terrorist. Contrary to what one might believe, however, the relationship between terrorism and democracy is not only genealogical but also ontological. Terrorism cannot be overcome once and for all; it remains carved into democracy, from which it can reemerge.

A glance back at the past shows that there has never been a time when democracy was not undermined by this uncomfortable traveling companion, which follows it stubbornly, adapts to its rhythms, adjusts to its forms, dogs its progress. Terrorism raises its flags where changes have been the most sweeping and deep, almost as if to indicate that democracy is moving too fast. Its actions are predisposed to emphasize imbalances and gaps; its attacks are aimed at undermining structures that are already shaky. Terrorism is an indicator of failed change, of a process such as globalization, which has foundered.

It is difficult to imagine that democracy could rid itself of this cumbersome burden. With its Quixotic incursions that produce perverse effects aimed at destabilizing democracy, terrorism does not succeed in truly threatening its existence; for its part, democracy, more exposed and more vulnerable than other political forms such as a dictatorship might be, possesses its own innate elasticity, which enables it to bend without falling apart. Democracy has proven to have an unexpected resiliency in the long term.

In targeting civilians, who are all equal in the face of its threat, terrorism directly touches citizens—the true representatives of a democratic state—who cannot help but feel unprotected, under attack, unarmed. The immediate temptation is to react by reinterpreting the laws that are in effect, or rather to twist them in order to be able to make extraordinary decisions. This is what the Bush administration did after the September 11 attacks, capitalizing on the shock that those attacks produced. The near future will tell whether what was considered to be the first democracy in the world made the right choice when it renounced many democratic prerogatives. What appears clear today is that, if democracy, in responding to terrorism, which violates its laws, violates its own laws as well—or, even more, ends up attacking itself—it will give in to its own autoimmune response and will self-destruct.

Democracy should admit that it does nothing more than open up a "space of freedom," a space in which it protects its secret, sheltered from any transparency. There it "saves and attends to even the most unexpected guest. The most foreign. Indeed, it is his land. It is generous, but also discreet."[24]

## 9   Snowden: on planetary surveillance

Among its most deleterious effects, the "war on terror" has produced a system of planetary surveillance. After having previously introduced provisions regarding cybersecurity, in 2008 the US government approved the FISA Amendments Act, which is still in effect as of this writing. This act authorized the National Security Agency (NSA) to gather, without a warrant, personal data on any foreigner; in the case of American citizens, it is easy for the agency to obtain a warrant.[25] Special programs such as PRISM and X-Keyscope have been developed—programs that make it possible to enter the portals of the main digital communities such as Apple, Google, Facebook, Skype, and YouTube and to intercept, with the tacit complicity of those service providers, any content or exchange, from e-mail to chat messages, with no restrictions. The NSA has thus been able to monitor, analyze, and archive global electronic communications, treating anyone who goes online as a potential suspect. This kind of surveillance makes transparent private lives that are conducted online, so that everyone is not only visible but also locatable. The *New York Times* revealed that, starting in 2010, the NSA has begun to compile profiles on every inhabitant of the planet.[26]

This gigantic network, in which everyone is surveilled and monitored by an invisible power, is the most recent and the most alarming version of the Panopticon, with the difference that Jeremy Bentham's project was conceived for a prison. But the panoptic surveillance of the West does not need to design a system of cells for everyone to have the impression of being constantly watched by an immense, all-seeing eye. To dominate means to see without being seen, remaining hidden in the privilege of darkness, while those who are sentenced to be constantly observed know that they are being spied upon with no recourse.

This system of surveillance on a massive scale was exposed in June 2013 by Edward Snowden. After having placed his knowledge of telecommunications technology for years at the service of the CIA, where in 2007 he accessed top-secret information, Snowden began to have doubts about the scope and methods of electronic counterterrorism. After leaving the CIA, in 2009 Snowden began to work for Dell, a company known for producing personal computers; Dell subcontracted his services to the NSA. During that period, a large part of which he spent in Japan, Snowden was promoted to Dell's espionage division, which collects data and prepares for cyberattacks. After he returned to the United States in 2012, Snowden began to download all the files that he intended to divulge. In a risky, complicated operation, on May 20, 2013 he took a flight to Hong Kong, where he met several times with Laura Poitras, who filmed the meetings for the 2014 documentary film *Citizenfour*; also present at the meetings was Glenn Greenwald, who published Snowden's revelations in the daily newspaper *Guardian*.

The Snowden affair caused a big sensation, also because of its political repercussions. But nothing changed, even though evidence emerged that waging the "war on terror" is not the primary objective of planetary surveillance.

# 10   The new phobocracy

As security measures continue to multiply, the prolonged worldwide state of emergency seems to have left its mark in a profound, irreversible way on western democracy and on the national model that we have known up until now. Many have already warned that the end of the rule of law is looming. In the abstruse legislation on antiterrorism, where laws are often rewritten rather than suspended and where the exception quickly becomes the rule, it is possible to detect the advancing prow of a police state, the prosthesis of a bloodless sovereignty that does not know how and does not want to fade away.

The keyword in today's political lexicon has become "security." The "security state" is the model for a brand of politics that is reduced to mere administration, the exercise of governance that promises to reassure, protect, and defend its citizens; that is where it finds its legitimacy. Reasons of security have taken the place of "reason of state." Control, surveillance, and repression, understood in the broadest sense—even deterritorialized and digital—are part of the security state, which, however, remains uncharted territory, barely probed, hardly explored.

According to the etymology of the word—which comes from the Latin adjective *securus*, made up of *se-*, which has a privative value, and *cura*, meaning "care" or "concern"— "secure" means "without care" or "without worry." To be secure would mean to live without the shadow of looming threats, without having to be afraid of the future, without being prey to fear, hostage to terror—exactly the opposite of the condition of every citizen of the world today. The state promises what it cannot succeed in maintaining—security. Is this because there are innumerable questions, risks that are too high, a global scenario that is so complex? The state recognizes, in part, its own impotence. It succeeds in providing solutions, placating anxieties, facing new unknowns; it is not, however, capable of resolving all problems. And deep down, citizens should not expect it to do so. Ecological catastrophes, global disasters, economic uncertainty, and the precariousness of life appear to be ineluctable phenomena. In the name of the ironclad laws of economics as well as of those of history, the state abdicates; it abandons its citizens in the face of certain unforeseen events; it exposes them to certain dangers in order to deal with others, giving rise to a hierarchy of fears within which it puts into effect its security measures. Liberalism is the ideology of this abandonment. The promise of protection is limited, and always contains the threat of abandonment.

It is not by chance that promise and threat are connected. Indeed, they describe a perverse circle—the unprecedented, fear-inducing relationship in which the security state, in ensuring its citizens' safety, in protecting them, also holds them captive, chaining them to its own uncertain sovereignty. The traditional model outlined by Hobbes is overturned here. According to this model, the contract that transfers power to the sovereign presupposes reciprocal fear, everyone waging war against everyone else. The state intervenes to put an end to fear. But the reverse is true of the security state—here the state requires fear and is founded on fear. By definition, it is from fear that the state derives its legitimacy.

The suspicion—more than motivated—is that, in order to be legitimate, the state should cultivate fear, secretly foment it, intensify it through a daily political–mediatic orchestration. The obsession with security feeds on the "culture of fear." While it indicates the dangers that are gathering on the horizon—foreigners, the needy, refugees, immigrants, non-EU members, criminals, terrorists—the state proclaims: "Security comes first!" In the age of political disaffection, when there is no longer desire or emotional involvement, the only thing left is fear of a ubiquitous, undefined enemy to make depoliticized citizens emerge from the passivity that is immobilizing them. Thus individual fears, which otherwise divide and isolate people, eating away at connections, causing indifference, now cumulatively give rise to the phantasmic "we" of a community defined by fear that voluntarily submits to the security state.

It is no surprise that prevention is the standard-bearer of this new phobocracy. If a terrorist is one who "intimidates," if there are serious reasons to think that his or her behavior represents "a threat to public order," according to these indeterminate formulas that increasingly appear in laws that are enacted as emergency measures, then suspicion spreads and the range of preventative action extends beyond all proportion—because anyone, even if not a terrorist, could become one. What is targeted is not the act, but rather the possibility of the act. People think, hypothesize, conjecture, imagine—ending up by putting intentions rather than actions on trial. It is taken for granted that an act that is not carried out has been avoided only thanks to the preventative intervention of law enforcement.

Politics is replaced by policing, as the *possibility* of a terrorist act becomes confused with reality. The success of an operation that has neutralized a presumed terrorist act is praised. Nothing else is added—nor does public opinion ask for anything else. The name, personal details, and motives of the suspect—everything is nebulous. What is important is only the fact that a possible terrorist has been expelled, sent away, or imprisoned. Against every legal principle, certainty is renounced. The "version of the facts" is entrusted to the media, and to law enforcement, amid unreliable chatter and blatant contradictions. But the absence of certainty in the reconstruction of terrorist acts is nothing new. In fact, one is tempted to think that it is intentional. The more hazy and vague a terrorist's profile is, the more the threat remains obscure, and the more the terror looms and overwhelms.

Paradoxically, the security state turns out to be a state dominated by fear, a phobocracy that transmits alarm and dread, that spreads fear and anxiety. This means that not only does the state not stick to the promise that is inherent in its *raison d'être*—that is, to keep its citizens *sine cura*, without worry or care—it also leverages the terrorist threat by using fear as a tool, putting in motion that perverse cycle in which there should perhaps be read the hint of a new relationship of power, based on widespread, unlimited control, to which planetary surveillance is already tending. As systems of control multiply and procedures for the gathering of electronic data are refined, "security" is inexorably being transformed into an acute form of insecurity. In the process, there comes to light a systemic connection between the security state and terrorism. Without arriving at a "strategy of tension"—that is, at the extreme point of actually producing terror—the state still allows for terror to be produced. This explains the otherwise enigmatic choices that some western democracies have made, combatting terrorism internally but externally not precluding relationships with ambiguously compromised countries that have terrorist organizations, to which the democracies sell large quantities of arms.

To criminalize the *possibility* of a terrorist act means to permit a kind of preventative action that enables law enforcement and security forces to become the leading players in the "war on terror," giving them additional powers, while the powers of the judiciary are eclipsed and the margins of sovereignty erode. The imposing presence in large cities of law enforcement units, as well as of military personnel, attests to the porousness of the boundaries between criminal and enemy, between internal violence and urban warfare, demonstrating how the "war on terror" is a police operation on a planetary scale. Suspense and tension are the earmarks of an armed vigilance, a permanent vigil, a constant wakefulness on the part of law enforcement and security forces—which nevertheless, like every form of insomnia, cannot help but produce nightmares, delirium, obnubilations, hallucinations. Anxiety predominates, suspicion is everywhere: every citizen becomes a potential terrorist. While the security state moves away from politics, venturing toward unknown territory, the police and the armed forces reveal their spectral face, showing what they truly are: not the armed branch of the state, but the original accessory of sovereignty.

Destined for decades to a dignified decline beneath the cloudy skies of globalization, impaired and handicapped in its functions, the nation-state, now almost incapable of decreeing laws, appears increasingly delegitimized; it reacts with vehemence, searching for any kind of surreptitious sovereignty, even if it is a supplement, a sort of prosthesis. The "war on terror," with all the bogeymen that it raises—from the invasion of immigrants to the clash of civilizations—gives nation-states the opportunity to restore the faith of their citizens, to make their hostility converge upon a common enemy, to rebuild their armor. This is the origin of the extreme autoimmune reaction with which, in order to eliminate the virus of terrorism, the nation-state ends up ripping apart its own body, laying waste to the lives of its citizens. Its armor is the new phobocracy—the power of terror wielded by a sovereign armed force. The vagaries of globalization have not spared sovereignty but in fact have made it waver, prompting it to use artifices, prostheses, accessories, and even to engage in violence, shows of force, its own brand of terror. It would be better to renounce every form of sovereignty in an unconditional, definitive way.

# Notes

## Notes to Chapter 1

1 Theodor W. Adorno, *Negative Dialectics*, trans. E. B. Ashton (New York: Continuum, 2007), 320.
2 [TN: A suburb in south Brussels.]
3 [TN: Visit https://www.cnbc.com/2015/11/13/obama-france-attack-is-on-all-of-humanity-and-universal-values-we-share.html.]
4 Antoine Leiris, *You Will Not Have My Hate*, trans. Sam Taylor (New York: Penguin Books, 2016), 14.
5 Frédéric Gros, *States of Violence: An Essay on the End of War*, trans. Krzystof Fijalkowski (London: Seagull Books, 2010).
6 Carlo Galli, *Political Spaces and Global War*, trans. Elisabeth Fay (Minneapolis: University of Minnesota Press, 2010).
7 Carl von Clausewitz, *On War*, trans. Michael Howard and Peter Paret (Princeton, NJ: Princeton University Press, 1988), 605 (from Book 8).
8 Carl Schmitt, *The Concept of the Political*, trans. George Schwab (Chicago, IL: University of Chicago Press, 2007), 94.
9 Martin Heidegger, *Ponderings XII-XI: Black Notebooks 1939-1941*, trans. Richard Rojcewicz (Bloomington: Indiana University Press, 2017), §114, 110.
10 Carl Schmitt, *Theory of the Partisan: Intermediate Commentary on the Concept of the Political*, trans. G. L. Ulmen (New York: Telos Press, 2007), 94–95.
11 Hannah Arendt, *On Revolution* (New York: Viking, 2006), 11.

12 Giorgio Agamben, *Stasis: Civil War as a Political Paradigm*, trans. Nicholas Heron (Stanford, CA: Stanford University Press, 2015), 22.

13 Theodor Adorno, *Minima Moralia: Reflections on a Damaged Life*, trans. E. F. N. Jephcott (London/New York: Verso, 2005), 234–5; Hannah Arendt, "Organized Guilt and Universal Responsibility," in Peter Baehr, ed., *The Portable Hannah Arendt* (New York: Penguin, 2000), 146–56.

14 See Jean-François Lyotard, *The Postmodern Condition: A Report on Knowledge*, trans. Geoff Bennington and Brian Massumi (Minneapolis: University of Minnesota Press, 1984).

15 Jürgen Habermas, "Die Moderne: Ein unvollendetes Projekt," *Die Zeit*, September 19, 1980 (https://www.zeit.de/1980/39/die-moderne-ein-unvollendetes-projekt).

16 See Roberto Esposito, *A Philosophy for Europe: from the Outside*, trans. Zakiya Hanafi (Cambridge: Polity, 2018).

17 Giovanna Borradori, ed., *Philosophy in a Time of Terror: Dialogues with Jürgen Habermas and Jacques Derrida* (Chicago, IL: University of Chicago Press, 2003), 30.

18 Ibid., 92.

19 See ibid., 95 ff.

20 Jean Baudrillard, *The Spirit of Terrorism*, trans. Chris Turner (New York: Verso, 2012), 30.

21 Jean Baudrillard, *The Transparency of Evil: Essays on Extreme Phenomena*, trans. James Benedict (London: Verso, 2009), 75 ff.

22 Paul Virilio, *Pure War*, trans. Mark Polizzotti, revised edition with a new introduction by Sylvère Lotringer and Paul Virilio (Los Angeles, CA: Semiotext(e), 2008).

23 Jean Baudrillard, "Figures of the Transpolitical," in idem, *Fatal Strategies*, trans. P. Beitchman and W. G. J. Niesluchowski (Los Angeles, CA: Semiotext(e), 2008), 65.

24 Jean Baudrillard, *Utopia Deferred: Writings from "Utopie" (1967–1978)*, trans. Stuart Kendall (New York: Semiotext(e), 2007), 243.

25 Michel Deutsch, *La Décennie rouge: Une histoire allemande* (Paris: Christian Bourgois, 2007), 127–9.

26 Baudrillard, *Utopia Deferred*, 302.

27 Jean Beaudrillard, *Power Inferno: Requiem pour les Twin Towers* (Paris: Galilée, 2002), 55.

28 Peter Sloterdijk, *Foams: Spheres*, vol. 3: *Plural Spherology*, trans. Wieland Hoban (Los Angeles, CA: Semiotext(e), 2016), 103 .

29 Wolfgang Sofsky, *The Order of Terror: The Concentration Camp*, trans. William Templer (Princeton, NJ: Princeton University Press, 1997).

30 Sloterdijk, *Foams*, 128: "Churchill was willing, at least, to term himself a terrorist."
31 [TN: This is a reference to Heidegger's cabin in the Black Forest.]
32 Sloterdijk, *Foams*, 100.
33 Ibid., 116.
34 Peter Sloterdijk, *Rage and Time*, trans. Mario Wenning (New York: Columbia University Press, 2012), 218.
35 See chapter 2, section 8 in this book.

# Notes to Chapter 2

1 Quoted in Frédéric de Towarnicki, *Ernst Jünger, Récit d'un passeur de siècle: rencontres et conversations* (Monaco: Éditions du Rocher, 2000), 41.
2 See Noam Chomsky and André Vltchek, *On Western Terrorism from Hiroshima to Drone Warfare* (London: Pluto Press, 2017); and, from an even earlier period, see Albert Camus, *The Rebel: An Essay on Man in Revolt*, trans. Anthony Bower (New York: Vintage, 2012).
3 As has been done by Michael Walzer in *Just and Unjust Wars: A Moral Argument with Historical Illustrations* (New York: Basic Books, 2015), 250 ff.
4 Walter Laqueur, *A History of Terrorism* (London: Taylor & Francis, 2017), 79.
5 Walter Laqueur, *The New Terrorism: Fanaticism and the Arms of Mass Destruction* (New York: Oxford University Press, 2002), 156 ff.
6 Gérard Chaliand and Arnaud Blin, eds., *The History of Terrorism: From Antiquity to Al Qaeda*, trans. Edward Schneider, Kathryn Pulver, and Jesse Browner (Berkeley: University of California Press, 2007), 5.
7 François Heisbourg, *Hyperterrorisme: La nouvelle guerre* (Paris: Éditions Odile Jacob, 2001).
8 Chaliand and Blin, *History of Terrorism*, 59.
9 [TN: The description "white weapon" (*arma bianca*) seems to correspond, in several languages, to a generic term for weapons that are not of the firing type.]
10 For a critique, see Jacques Sémelin, *Purify and Destroy: The Political Uses of Massacre and Genocide*, trans. Cynthia Schoch (New York: Columbia University Press, 2007), 359.
11 Didier Bigo, "L'impossible cartographie du terrorisme," *Cultures et conflits*, February 25, 2005, 2–6.

12 Charles Townshend, *Terrorism: A Very Short Introduction* (Oxford: Oxford University Press), 3.
13 Martin Heidegger, *Being and Time*, trans. Joan Stambaugh (Albany: SUNY Press, 2010), 178 ff.
14 Thomas Hobbes, *Leviathan: With Selected Variants from the Latin edition of 1668*, ed. Edwin Curley (Indianapolis, IN: Hackett, 1994), 89.
15 Immanuel Kant, *The Conflict of the Faculties*, trans. Mary J. Gregor (Lincoln, NE: University of Nebraska Press, 1992), 145, 143.
16 Georg Wilhelm Friedrich Hegel, *Phenomenology of Spirit*, trans. A.V. Miller (Oxford: Oxford University Press, 2013), §590, 359.
17 Hannah Arendt, "Ideology and Terror: A Novel Form of Government," in eadem, *Totalitarianism: Part Three of the Origins of Totalitarianism* (San Diego, CA: Harcourt Brace Jovanovich, 1985), 158–78, esp. 164.
18 Ibid., 173.
19 Max Horkheimer, "Politik und Soziales," in Alfred Schmidt and Gunelin Schmid Noerr, eds., *Gesammelte Schriften VIII: Vorträge und Aufzeichnungen 1949–1973* (Frankfurt: Fischer Verlag, 1985), 46.
20 See chapter 4, section 10 in this book.
21 Edmund Burke, *Letters on a Regicide Peace* (London: Payne, 1795), 315.
22 Arnaud Blin, *Le Terrorisme* (Paris: Le Cavalier Bleu, 2005), 25. This equation between Terror and terrorism also appears in widely disseminated texts, as well as in dictionaries and encyclopedias.
23 See Chaliand and Blin, *History of Terrorism*, 98.
24 Sophie Wahnich, *In Defence of the Terror: Liberty or Death in the French Revolution*, trans. David Fernbach (London: Verso, 2015), 8.
25 Hannah Arendt, *On Revolution* (New York: Penguin Books, 2006), 90.
26 *Le Moniteur universel*, reprint (Paris: Plon, 1947), vol. 17, 526.
27 Remo Bodei, *Geometry of the Passions: Fear, Hope, Happiness: Philosophy and Political Use*, trans. Gianpiero W. Doebler (Toronto: University of Toronto Press, 2018), 382.
28 George Büchner, *Danton's Death*, Act 1, scene V, in idem, *Complete Plays and Prose*, trans. Carl Richard Mueller (New York: Hill and Wang, 1985), 19.
29 Louis Antoine de Saint-Just, *Rapport au nom du Comité de salut public et du Comité de sûreté général sur les personnes*

*incarcérées*, in idem, *Oeuvres complètes* (Paris: Gallimard, 2004), 700.

30 See Patrice Gueniffey, *La Politique de la terreur: Essai sur la violence révolutionnaire, 1789–1794* (Paris: Gallimard, 2000), 149 ff.

31 Walter Benjamin, "Critique of Violence," in idem, *Reflections: Essays, Aphorisms, Autobiographical Writings*, trans. Edmund Jephcott (New York: Schocken Books, 2007), 297 ff.

32 John Keegan, "Why the New Terrorism Threatens All of Humanity," *Telegraph*, October 25, 2001 (https://www.telegraph.co.uk/comment/4266434/Why-the-new-terrorism-threatens-all-of-humanity.html).

33 Olivier Roy, *Jihad and Death: The Global Appeal of the Islamic State*, trans. Cynthia Schoch (London: Hurst, 2017), 5–6.

34 André Glucksmann, *Dostoïevski à Manhattan* (Paris: Robert Laffont, 2002), 80, 82: *du terroriste come ennemi de l'humanité; cela fonde en droit une alliance universelle contre la terrorisme.*

35 Friedrich Nietzsche, *The Joyful Wisdom: La gaya scienza*, trans. Thomas Common (New York: Ungar, 1960), §125.

36 Friedrich Nietzsche, *The Will to Power: An Attempted Transvaluation of All Values*, vols. 1–2, trans. Anthony M. Ludovici (Overland Park, KS: Digireads, 2010), location 296.

37 Ibid., location 232.

38 Ibid., location 376.

39 Ibid., location 957.

40 Martin Heidegger, *The Question of Being*, trans. William Kluback and Jean J. Wilde (New Haven, CT: Twayne, 1958), 49: "Perhaps the zero line is suddenly emerging before us in the form of a planetary catastrophe."

41 Ivan Turgenev, *Fathers and Sons*, trans. Constance Garnett (Lawrence, KS: Digireads, 2017), 20.

42 Ivan Turgenev, *Literary Reminiscences and Autobiographical Fragments*, trans. David Magarshack (New York: Farrar, Straus and Cahady, 1958), 200.

43 Sergey Nechayev, "The Duties of the Revolutionary toward Himself," in idem, *The Revolutionary Catechism*, no. 1. Marxist Archive (https://www.marxists.org/subject/anarchism/nechayev/catechism.htm).

44 Ibid., no. 6.

45 Franco Venturi, *Roots of Revolution: A History of the Populist and Socialism Movements in 19th Century Russia*, trans. Francis Haskell (London: Phoenix Press, 2001), 45.

46 Georges Ribeill, ed., *Marx/Bakounine: socialisme autoritaire ou libertaire?* (Paris: Union Générale d'Éditions, 1985), vol. II, 119–21.

47 Uri Eisenzweig, *Fictions de l'anarchisme* (Paris: Christian Bourgois, 2001), 54ff.

48 Fyodor Dostoyevsky, *The Brothers Karamazov*, trans. Constance Garnett (Overland Park, KS: Digireads, 2017), 222.

49 Fyodor Dostoyevsky, *A Writer's Diary*, trans. Kenneth Lantz (Evanston, IL: Northwestern University Press, 2009), 64–5.

50 Friedrich Nietzsche, *The Twilight of the Idols with the Antichrist and Ecce Homo*, trans. Antony M. Ludovici (Hertfordshire: Wordsworth Editions Limited, 2013), §45, "The criminal and his like."

51 Fyodor Dostoyevsky, "One of Today's Falsehoods," in idem, *A Writer's Diary*, trans. Kenneth Lantz (Evanston, IL: Northwestern University Press, 2009), 67–8.

52 Vladimir Ilyich Lenin, "Letter to American Workers," trans. Jim Riordan. Marxist Internet Archive (https://www.marxists.org/archive/lenin/works/1918/aug/20.htm).

53 [TN: The soviets were governmental organizations during the Russian Revolution.]

54 Vladimir Ilyich Lenin, "'Harmonious Organisation' and Dictatorship," Section 7 of "The Immediate Tasks of the Soviet Government," trans. Clemens Dutt. Marxist Internet Archive (https://www.marxists.org/archive/lenin/works/1918/mar/x03.htm). Originally published on April 28, 1918 in *Pravda* No. 83 and *Izvestia VTsIK* No. 85.

55 Carl Schmitt, *Dictatorship: From the Origin of the Modern Concept of Sovereignty to the Proletarian Class-Struggle*, trans. Michael Hoelzl and Graham Ward (Cambridge: Polity, 2017), 112 ff.

56 [TN: The 'past' referred to here is the Mexican revolution depicted in the film.]

57 Visit https://aphelis.net/please-dont-about-revolutions-fistful-dynamite-sergio-leone-1971.

58 [TN: Mao Tse-tung, "Report on an Investigation of the Peasant Movement in Hunan," March 1927. In idem, *Selected Works*, vol. 1. Marxists Internet Archive (https://www.marxists.org/reference/archive/mao/selected-works/volume-1/mswv1_2.htm).]

59 Carl Schmitt, *The Concept of the Political*, trans. George Schwab (Chicago, IL: University of Chicago Press, 2007), 29.

60 Carl Schmitt, *Theory of the Partisan: Intermediate Commentary on the Concept of the Political*, trans. G. L. Ulmen (New York: Telos Press, 2007), 20 ff.

61 Ibid., 71.
62 Ernesto Che Guevara, *Guerrilla Warfare*, trans. J. P. Morray (Melbourne: Ocean Press, 2006), 52, 19.
63 Schmitt, *Theory of the Partisan*, 89.
64 Ibid., 94.

# Notes to Chapter 3

1 Farhad Khosrokhavar, *Radicalization: Why Some People Choose the Path of Violence*, trans. Jane Marie Todd (New York: New Press, 2016), 1 ff.
2 Martin Heidegger, *Letter on Humanism*, trans. Frank A. Capuzzi, in idem, *Basic Writings*, ed. by David Farrell Krell (New York: Harper Perennial, 2008), 213–66, esp. 243: "Homelessness is coming to be the destiny of the world." See also Donatella Di Cesare, "Esilio e globalizzazione," *Iride* 54 (2008), 273–86.
3 See chapter 4, section 2 in this book.
4 Abu Jihad al-Masri, *The Management of Savagery: The Most Critical Stage through Which the Islamic Nation Will Pass* (https://azelin.files.wordpress.com/2010/08/abu-bakr-naji-the-management-of-savagery-the-most-critical-stage-through-which-the-umma-will-pass.pdf).
5 Tahar Ben Jelloun, "Le Califat sauvage," in Éric Fottorino, ed., *Qui est Daech? Comprendre le nouveau terrorisme* (Paris: Philippe Rey, 2015), 12.
6 Sayyid Quṭb, *In the Shade of the Qur'an*, trans. M. A. Salahi, A.A. Shamis, and Adil Salahi (Leicester: Islamic Foundation, 1998–2006).
7 See Jean-Pierre Filiu, *Apocalypse in Islam*, trans. M. B. DeBevoise (Berkeley: University of California Press, 2011).
8 See David Cook, *Contemporary Muslim Apocalyptic Literature* (Syracuse, NY: Syracuse University Press, 2008), 174 ff.
9 John Updike, *Terrorist: A Novel* (New York: Random House, 2006).
10 It is estimated that at least 40 percent of those who have become radical Islamists are converts.
11 Khosrokhavar, *Radicalization*, 96 ff.
12 See chapter 4, section 3 in this book.
13 See Slavoj Žižek, *Welcome to the Desert of the Real: Five Essays on September 11 and Related Dates* (London: Verso, 2013), 91.
14 Roberto Esposito, *Bios: Biopolitics and Philosophy*, trans. Timothy Campbell (Minneapolis: University of Minnesota

Press, 2008), 110ff. By the same author, see *Immunitas: The Protection and Negation of Life*, trans. Zakiya Hanafi (Cambridge: Polity Press, 2011).

15 Daniel Boyarin, *Dying for God: Martyrdom and the Making of Christianity and Judaism* (Stanford, CA: Stanford University Press, 1999).

16 [TN: This is a noun borrowed in postclassical Latin from the ancient Greek *martus* (μάρτυς) "witness."]

17 *City of God*, Book 1, ch. 17.

18 See Farhad Khosrokhavar, *Suicide Bombers: Allah's New Martyrs*, trans. David Macey (London: Pluto Press, 2005), 6 ff.

19 In the Muslim world, the Shia are a minority by comparison to the Sunni. For an overview, see Moojan Momen, *An Introduction to Shi'i Islam: History and Doctrines of Twelver Shi'ism* (New Haven, CT: Yale University Press, 1987).

20 Giorgio Agamben, *Homo Sacer: Sovereign Power and Bare Life*, trans. Daniel Heller-Roazen (Stanford, CA: Stanford University Press, 1998).

21 Jean Baudrillard, *The Transparency of Evil: Essays on Extreme Phenomena*, trans. James Benedict (London: Verso, 2009), 75.

22 Raymond Aron, *Peace and War: A Theory of International Relations* (New Brunswick, NJ: Transaction Publishers, 2003), 170.

23 See Susan Sontag, *Regarding the Pain of Others* (New York: Farrar, Straus and Giroux 2003), 84 ff.

24 See, for example, the now-defunct online magazine *Dabiq*, the Islamic State News (ISN), and the online magazine *Dar-al-Islam*, which are sometimes blacked out or censored.

25 Mike Davis, *Buda's Wagon: A Brief History of the Car Bomb* (London: Verso, 2017), especially ch. 2.

26 [TN: Pejorative nickname for the Lehi, a Hebrew militant group.]

27 Ibid., location 180 (e-book).

28 Ibid., location 279.

29 Elias Canetti, *The Conscience of Words*, trans. Joachim Neugroschel (New York: Seabury Press, 1979), 13.

30 On the systematic violence of torture, see Donatella Di Cesare, *Torture* (Cambridge: Polity, 2018).

31 Jethro Mullen, "Beheading of American Journalist James Foley Recalls Past Horrors," CNN, August 20, 2014 (http://www.cnn.com/2014/08/20/world/meast/journalist-beheadings/index.html).

32 Philippe-Joseph Salazar, *Words Are Weapons: Inside ISIS's Rhetoric of Terror*, trans. Dorna Khazeni (New Haven, CT: Yale University Press, 2017), 117 ff.

33 Judith Butler, *Precarious Life: The Powers of Mourning and Violence* (London: Verso, 2004), 19 ff., and *Giving an Account of Oneself* (New York: Fordham University Press, 2005), 83 ff.

34 Adriana Cavarero, *Horrorism: Naming Contemporary Violence*, trans. William McCuaig, 30 ff.

35 See Richard Rechtman, "L'Ambition génocidaire de Daech," in Nicolas Truong, ed., *Résister à la terreur* (Paris: Le Monde-Nouvelles Éditions de l'Aube, 2016), 105–11.

36 Soren Seelow, "C'est Charlie, venez vite, ils sont tous morts," *Le Monde*, January 13, 2015 (http://www.lemonde.fr/societe/article/2015/01/13/c-est-charlie-venez-vite-ils-sont-tous-morts_4554839_3224.html).

37 See Marion van Renterghem, "Les Frères Kouachi: une jeunesse française," *Le Monde*, February 13, 2015 (http://www.lemonde.fr/societe/article/2015/02/12/les-freres-kouachi-une-jeunesse-francaise_4575115_3224.html).

38 [TN: Unidentifed quotation.]

39 Emmanuel Levinas, *Otherwise than Being or Beyond Essence*, trans. Alphonso Lingis (Dorcrecht: Springer Netherlands, 2010), 112.

40 Ibid., 117.

41 Emmanuel Levinas, *Totality and Infinity: An Essay on Exteriority*, trans. Alphonso Lingis (Dordrecht: Kluwer Academic Publishers, 2011), 198.

42 Giovanna Borradori, ed., *Philosophy in a Time of Terror: Dialogues with Jürgen Habermas and Jacques Derrida* (Chicago, IL: University of Chicago Press, 2003), 97. Italics are mine.

# Notes to Chapter 4

1 Régis Debray, "Le Passage à l'infini," in Catherine Lavenir and François-Bernard Huyghe, eds., *La Scène terroriste* (Les Cahiers de médiologie 13) (Paris: Gallimard, 2002), 13.

2 Michael Watts, "Revolutionary Islam: A Geography of Modern Terror," in Derek Gregory and Allan Pred, eds., *Violent Geographies: Fear, Terror, and Political Violence* (New York: Routledge, 2007), 198.

3 Arjun Appadurai, *Fear of Small Numbers: An Essay on the Geography of Anger* (Durham, NC: Duke University Press, 2006), 115ff. See also Samuel P. Huntington, *The Clash of*

*Civilizations and the Remaking of World Order* (New York: Simon & Schuster, 2011).

4  Slavoj Žižek, *Welcome to the Desert of the Real: Five Essays on September 11 and Related Dates* (London: Verso, 2013), 52.

5  James Hillman, A *Terrible Love of War* (New York: Penguin, 2004), 178 ff.

6  See Jan Assmann, *Of God and Gods: Egypt, Israel, and the Rise of Monotheism* (Madison: University of Wisconsin Press, 2008), and *The Price of Monotheism*, trans. Robert Savage (Stanford, CA: Stanford University Press, 2010).

7  Peter Sloterdijk, *God's Zeal: The Battle of the Three Monotheisms*, trans. Wieland Hoban (Cambridge: Polity, 2009), and *In the Shadow of Mount Sinai*, trans. Wieland Hoban (Cambridge: Polity, 2016). Jacques Derrida, "Faith and Knowledge: The Two Sources of 'Religion' at the Limits of Reason Alone," trans. Samuel Weber, in Jacques Derrida and Gianni Vattimo, eds., *Religion* (Cambridge: Polity, 1998), 1–78.

8  Olivier Roy, *Holy Ignorance: When Religion and Culture Part Ways*, trans. Ros Schwartz (Oxford: Oxford University Press, 2013), 23.

9  Michael Löwy, "Opium du peuple? Marxisme critique et religion," *Contretemps* 12 (2010) (http://www.contretemps.eu/opium-peuple-marxisme-critique-religion).

10 Karl Marx, *Critique of Hegel's "Philosophy of Right,"* trans. Annette Jolin and Joseph O'Malley (Cambridge: Cambridge University Press, 1970), 131.

11 Karl Marx, *Das Kapital: A Critique of Political Economy*, trans. Samuel Moore (Seattle, WA: Pacific Publishing Studio, 2010), 18 ff. (digital edition).

12 Jacques Derrida, *Specters of Marx: The State of the Debt, The Work of Mourning and the New International*, trans. Peggy Kamuf (New York: Routledge, 2006), 130.

13 Jean-Yves Calez, "La religion et la politique," in *Marx et le marxisme: une pensée, une histoire* (Paris: Eyrolles, 2007), 39 ff.

14 Jean Birnbaum, *Un silence religieux: la gauche face au djihadisme* (Paris: Seuil, 2016), 144 ff.

15 Michel Foucault, *Taccuino persiano*, ed. by Renzo Guolo and Pierluigi Panza (Milan: Guerrini e Associati, 1998), 63.

16 Slavoj Žižek, "Michel Foucault and the Iranian Event," in idem, *In Defense of Lost Causes* (London: Verso, 2009), 107 ff.

17 Chris Harman, *The Prophet and the Proletariat: Islamic Fundamentalism, Class, and Revolution* (London: Socialist Workers Party, 1999), 56. Also available online at http://www.marxists.de/religion/harman.

18 Gilbert Achcar, *Marxism, Orientalism, Cosmopolitanism* (Chicago, IL: Haymarket Books, 2013), 25.

19 Étienne Balibar, *Saeculum: culture, religion, idéologie* (Paris: Galilée, 2012), 51 ff.

20 Francis Fukuyama, *The End of History and the Last Man* (London: Hamish Hamilton, 1992).

21 Walter Benjamin, "Capitalism as Religion [Fragment 74]," trans. Chad Kautzer, in Eduardo Mendieta, ed., *The Frankfurt School on Religion: Key Writings by the Major Thinkers* (New York: Routledge, 2005), 259.

22 Mohamedou Ould Slahi, *Guantánamo Diary*, ed. by Larry Siems (New York: Little, Brown, 2015).

23 Jacques Follorou, *Démocraties sous contrôle: La victoire posthume d'Oussama Ben Laden* (Paris: CNRS, 2014), 9. See also "Bin Laden's Sole Post-September 11 TV Interview Aired," CNN, February 5, 2002 (http://edition.cnn.com/2002/US/01/31/gen.binladen.interview).

24 Roberto Esposito, *Dieci pensieri sulla politica*, rev. edn. (Bologna: Il Mulino, 2011), 74.

25 FISA stands for Foreign Intelligence Surveillance Act. [TN: see https://www.govtrack.us/congress/bills/110/hr6304/text.]

26 James Risen and Laura Poitras, "NSA Gathers Data on Social Connections of US Citizens," *New York Times*, September 28, 2013 (https://www.nytimes.com/2013/09/29/us/nsa-examines-social-networks-of-us-citizens.html).

# Selected Bibliography

Ackerman, Bruce. *Before the Next Attack: Preserving Civil Liberties in an Age of Terrorism*. New Haven, CT: Yale University Press, 2006.

Adonis. *Violence and Islam: Conversations with Houria Abdelouahed*. Translated by David Watson. Cambridge: Polity, 2016.

Agamben, Giorgio. *Homo Sacer: Sovereign Power and Bare Life*. Translated by Daniel Heller-Roazen. Stanford, CA: Stanford University Press, 1998.

Agamben, Giorgio. *Stasis: Civil War as a Political Paradigm*. Translated by Nicholas Heron. Stanford, CA: Stanford University Press, 2015.

Asad, Talal. *On Suicide Bombing*. New York: Columbia University Press, 2007.

Augé, Marc. *Journal de guerre*. Paris: Galilée, 2002.

Badiou, Alain. *Our Wound Is Not So Recent: Thinking the Paris Killings of 13 November*. Translated by Robin Mackay. Cambridge: Polity, 2016.

Baudrillard, Jean. *Power Inferno: Requiem pour les Twin Towers*. Paris: Galilée, 2002.

Baudrillard, Jean. *The Spirit of Terrorism*. Translated by Chris Turner. New York: Verso, 2012.

Baudrillard, Jean. *The Transparency of Evil: Essays on Extreme Phenomena*. Translated by James Benedict. London: Verso, 2009.

Baudrillard, Jean, and Edgar Morin. *La Violence du monde*. Paris: Éditions du Félin, 2003.

Ben Jelloun, Tahar. *Le Terrorisme expliqué à nos enfants*. Paris: Éditions du Seuil, 2016.

Benslama, Fethi. *Un furieux désir de sacrifice: Le surmusulman*. Paris: Éditions du Seuil, 2016.

Benslama, Fethi, ed. *L'Idéal et la cruauté: Subjectivité et politique de la radicalisation*. Paris: Lignes, 2015.

Berman, Paul. *Terror and Liberalism*. New York: W. W. Norton, 2004.

Berti, Benedetta. *La fine del terrorismo: Oltre l'ISIS e lo stato d'emergenza*. Milan: Mondadori, 2017.

Biancheri, Boris, ed. *Il nuovo disordine globale dopo l'11 settembre*. Milan: Università Bocconi Editore, 2002.

Blin, Arnaud, and Gérard Chaliand, *The History of Terrorism: From Antiquity to ISIS* (updated edn., with a new preface and final chapter). Translated by Edward Schneider, Kathryn Pulver, and Jesse Browner. Oakland, CA: University of California Press, 2016.

Bonante, Luigi. *Terrorismo internazionale*. Florence: Giunti-Casterman, 1994.

Borradori, Giovanna, ed. *Philosophy in a Time of Terror: Dialogues with Jürgen Habermas and Jacques Derrida*. Chicago, IL: University of Chicago Press, 2003.

Campanini, Massimo. *An Introduction to Islamic Philosophy*. Translated by Caroline Higgett. Edinburgh: Edinburgh University Press, 2008.

Campanini, Massimo. *Philosophical Perspectives on Modern Qur'anic Exegesis: Key Paradigms and Concepts*. Bristol, CT: Equinox, 2016.

Campanini, Massimo. *The Qur'an: Modern Muslim Interpretations*. Translated by Caroline Higget. London: Routledge, 2011.

Campanini, Massimo. *Reading the Qu'ran in the Modern World*. London: Routledge, 2010.

Carbone, Mauro. *Essere morti insieme: L'evento dell'11 settembre 2001*. Turin: Bollati Boringhieri, 2007.

Cavarero, Adriana. *Horrorism: Naming Contemporary Violence*. Translated by William McCuaig. New York: Columbia University Press, 2009.

Chomsky, Noam. *9–11: Was There an Alternative? With a New Essay Written after the Assassination of Osama Bin Laden*. New York: Seven Stories Press, 2011.

Chomsky, Noam, and André Vltchek. *On Western Terrorism from Hiroshima to Drone Warfare* (new edn.). London: Pluto Press, 2017.

Curi, Umberto. *I figli di Ares: Guerra infinita e terrorismo*. Rome: Castelvecchi, 2016.

Décugis, Jean-Michel, François Malye, and Jérôme Vincent. *Les Coulisses du 13 novembre*. Paris: Plan, 2016.

Derrida, Jacques. "Faith and Knowledge: The Two Sources of 'Religion' at the Limits of Reason Alone," translated by Samuel Weber. In Jacques Derrida and Gianni Vattimo, eds., *Religion: Cultural Memory in the Present* (1–78). Cambridge: Polity, 1998.

Derrida, Jacques. *Specters of Marx: The State of the Debt, the Work of Mourning and the New International*. Translated by Peggy Kamuf. New York: Routledge, 2006.

Deutsch, Michel. *La Décennie rouge: Une histoire allemande*. Paris: Christian Bourgois, 2007.

Di Cesare, Donatella. *Torture*. Translated by David Broder. Cambridge: Polity, 2018.

Duque, Félix. *Terror tras la postmodernidad*. Madrid: Abada Editores, 2008.

Eisenzweig, Uri. *Fictions de l'anarchisme*. Paris: Christian Bourgois, 2001.

Eltahawy, Mona. "Why Do They Hate Us? The Real War on Women Is in the Middle East." *Foreign Policy*, April 23, 2012.

Enzensberger, Hans Magnus. "The Radical Loser." Translated by Nicholas Grindell. signandsight.com, January 12, 2005. http://www.signandsight.com/features/493.html.

Erelle, Anna. *In the Skin of a Jihadist: A Young Journalist Enters the ISIS Recruitment Network*. Translated by Erin Potter. New York: Harper Collins, 2015.

Esposito, Roberto. *Immunitas: The Protection and Negation of Life*. Translated by Zakiya Hanafi. Cambridge: Polity, 2011.

Ferragu, Giles. *Histoire du terrorisme*. Paris: Perrin, 2014.

Filiu, Jean-Pierre. *Apocalypse in Islam*. Translated by M. B. DeBevoise. Berkeley: University of California Press, 2011.

Flores d'Arcais, Paolo. *La guerra del sacro: Terrorismo, laicità e democrazia radicale*. Milan: Cortina, 2016.

Follorou, Jacques. *Démocraties sous contrôle: La victoire posthume d'Oussama Ben Laden*. Paris: CNRS, 2014.

Fottorino Éric, ed. *Qui est Daesh? Comprendre le nouveau terrorisme*. Paris: Le 1/Philippe Rey, 2015.

Fukuyama, Francis. *The End of History and the Last Man*. London: Hamish Hamilton, 2012.

Gauchet, Marcel. *The Disenchantment of the World: A Political History of Religion*. Translated by Oscar Burge. Princeton, NJ: Princeton University Press, 1997.

Gauchet, Marcel. *La Religion dans la démocratie: Parcours de la laïcité*. Paris: Gallimard, 1998.

Gayraud, Jean-François, and David Sénat. *Le Terrorisme*. Paris: PUF, 2002.

Giglioli, Daniele. *All'ordine del giorno è il terrore*. Milan: Bompiani, 2007.

Giro, Mario. *Noi terroristi: Storie vere dal Nordafrica a Charlie Hebdo*. Milan: Guerrini e Associati, 2015.

Glucksmann, André. *Ouest contre Ouest*. Paris: Hachette, 2004.

Gray, John. *Al Qaeda and What It Means to Be Modern*. London: Faber & Faber, 2015.

Gros, Frédéric. *States of Violence: An Essay on the End of War*. Translated by Krzysztof Fijalkowski. London: Seagull Books, 2010.

Gueniffey, Patrice. *La Politique de la terreur: Essai sur la violence révolutionnaire, 1789–1794*. Paris: Gallimard, 2000.

Guevara, Che. *Guerrilla Warfare*. Translated by J. P. Morray. Melbourne: Ocean Press, 2006.

Guidére, Mathieu. *Terreur: La nouvelle ère: Des Twin Towers à Charlie*. Paris: Autrement, 2015.

Guolo, Renzo. *L'ultima utopia: Gli jihadisti europei*. Milan: Guerini e Associati, 2015.

Habermas, Jürgen. *The Divided West*. Translated by Ciaran Cronin. Cambridge: Polity, 2006.

Harman, Chris. *The Prophet and the Proletariat: Islamic Fundamentalism, Class, and Revolution* (rev. edn.). London: Socialist Workers Party, 1999. [The 1994 edition is available online at https://www.marxists.org/archive/harman/1994/xx/islam.htm]

Harris, Sam. *The End of Faith: Religion, Terror, and the Future of Reason*. New York: W. W. Norton, 2005.

Heisbourg, François. *Hyperterrorisme: La nouvelle guerre*. Paris: Éditions Odile Jacob, 2003.

Hénaff, Marcel. *Violence dans la raison? Conflit et cruauté*. Paris: L'Herne, 2014.

Horgan, John G. *The Psychology of Terrorism*. Abingdon: Routledge, 2014.

Huntington, Samuel P. *The Clash of Civilizations and the Remaking of World Order*. New York: Simon & Schuster, 2011.

Ianes, Dario, ed. *Parlare di ISIS ai bambini*. Trent: Centro Studi Erickson, 2016.

Juergensmeyer, Mark. *Terror in the Mind of God: The Global Rise of Religious Violence*. Berkeley: University of California Press, 2003.

Juzik, Julija. *Les Fiancées d'Allah: Le drame des femmes kamikazes tchétchènes*. Translated by Catherine Guetta. Paris: Presses de la Cité, 2005.

Kepel, Gilles. *Beyond Terror and Martyrdom: The Future of the Middle East*. Translated by Pascale Ghazaleh. Cambridge, MA: Harvard University Press, 2008.

Kepel, Gilles. *La Fracture*. Paris: Gallimard France Culture, 2016.

Kepel, Gilles. *Jihad: The Trail of Political Islam*. Translated by Anthony F. Roberts. London: Tauris, 2014.

Kepel, Gilles, with Antoine Jardin. *Terror in France: The Rise of Jihad in the West*. Princeton, NJ: Princeton University Press, 2017.

Khosrokhavar, Fahrad. *Suicide Bombers: Allah's New Martyrs*. Translated by David Macey. London: Pluto Press, 2005.

Laqueur, Walter. *The Age of Terrorism*. London: Transaction Publishers, 1997.

Laqueur, Walter. *No End to War: Terrorism in the Twenty-first Century*. New York: Continuum, 2007.

Laurens, Henry, and Mireille Delmas-Marty. *Terrorismes: Histoire et droit*. Paris: CNRS Éditions, 2010.

Malraux, André. *Le Triangle noir: Laclos, Goya, Saint-Just*. Paris: Le Monde, 1997.

Martelli, Michele. *Teologia del terrore: Filosofia, religione e politica dopo l'11 settembre*. Rome: manifestolibri, 2005.

Martin, Jean-Clément. *La Terreur: Part maudite de la Révolution*. Paris: Gallimard, 2010.

Merah, Abdelghani, with Mohamed Sifaoui. *Mon frère, ce terroriste: Un homme dénonce l'islamisme*. Paris: Calmann-Lévy, 2012.

Merleau-Ponty, Maurice. *Humanism and Terror: An Essay on the Communist Problem*. Translated and with a new introduction by John O'Neill. Abingdon: Routledge, 2017.

Momen, Moojan. *An Introduction to Shi'i Islam: The History and Doctrines of Twelver Shi'ism*. New Haven, CT: Yale University Press, 1987.

Muray, Philippe. *Chers djihadistes…* Paris: Éditions Mille et Une Nuits, 2002.

Napoleoni, Loretta. *ISIS: The Terror Nation*. New York: Seven Stories Press, 2017.

Neyrat, Frédéric. *Le Terrorisme: Un concept piégé*. Paris: Ère, 2011.

Ory, Pascal. *Ce que dit Charlie: Treize leçons d'histoire*. Paris: Gallimard, 2016.

Ould Slahi, Mohamedou. *Guantánamo Diary*. Edited by Larry Siems. New York: Little, Brown, 2015.

Rabinovitch, Gérard. *Terrorisme/Résistance: D'une confusion lexicale à l'époque des sociétés de masse*. Paris: Le Bord de l'eau, 2014.

Regazzoni, Simone. *Stato di legittima difesa: Obama e la filosofia della guerra al terrorismo*. Milan: Ponte alle Grazie, 2013.

Reuter, Christoph. *My Life Is a Weapon: A Modern History of Suicide Bombing*. Translated by Helene Ragg-Kirkby. Princeton, NJ: Princeton University Press, 2006.

Robin, Corey. *Fear: The History of a Political Idea*. New York: Oxford University Press, 2004.

Roy, Olivier. *Holy Ignorance: When Religion and Culture Part Ways*. Translated by Ros Schwartz. Oxford: Oxford University Press, 2013.

Roy, Olivier. *Jihad and Death: The Global Appeal of Islamic State*. Translated by Cynthia Schoch. London: Hurst, 2017.

Roy, Olivier. *La Peur de l'Islam: Dialogues avec Nicolas Truong*. La Tour d'Aigues: Éditions de l'Aube, 2015.

Sacco, Leonardo. *Kamikaze e Shahid: Linee guida per una comparazione storico-religiosa*. Rome: Bulzoni, 2005.

Salazar, Philippe-Joseph. *Words Are Weapons: Inside ISIS's Rhetoric of Terror*. Translated by Dorna Khazeni. New Haven, CT: Yale University Press, 2017.

Sémelin, Jacques. *Purify and Destroy: The Political Uses of Massacre and Genocide*. Translated by Cynthia Schoch. New York: Columbia University Press, 2007.

Sibony, Daniel. *Le grand malentendu: Islam, Israël, Occident*. Paris: Odile Jacob, 2015.

Sloterdijk, Peter. *Foams: Spheres*, vol. 3: *Plural Spherology*. Translated by Wieland Hoban. Los Angeles, CA: Semiotext(e), 2016.

Sloterdijk, Peter. *Rage and Time: A Psychopolitical Investigation*. Translated by Mario Wenning. New York: Columbia University Press, 2012.

Sofsky, Wolfgang. *Prinzip Sicherheit*. London: CreateSpace, 2016.

Sofsky, Wolfgang. *Violence: Terrorism, Genocide, War*. Translated by Anthea Bell. London: Granta, 2004.

Sommier, Isabelle. *Le Terrorisme*. Paris: Flammarion, 2000.

Stern, Jessica. *The Ultimate Terrorists*. Cambridge, MA: Harvard University Press, 2001.

Strada, Vittorio. *Etica del terrore: Da Fëdor Dostoevskij a Thomas Mann*. Florence: Liberal Libri, 2008.

Svendsen, Lars. *A Philosophy of Fear*. Translated by John Irons. London: Reaktion Books, 2009.

Terestchenko, Michel. *L'Ère des ténèbres*. Paris: Le Bord de l'eau, 2015.

Toscano, Roberto. *La violenza, le regole*. Turin: Einaudi, 2006.

Tosini, Domenico. *Terrorismo e antiterrorismo nel XXI secolo*. Rome: Laterza, 2007.

Townshend, Charles. *Terrorism: A Very Short Introduction*. Oxford: Oxford University Press, 2011.

Truong, Nicholas, ed. *Résister à la terreur*. Paris: Le Monde/Éditions de l'Aube, 2016.

Vallat, David. *Terreur de jeunesse: Le témoignage d'un ex-djihadiste*. Paris: Calmann-Lévy, 2016.

Walther, Rudolph. "Terror, Terrorismus." In Otto Brunner, Werner Conze, and Reinhart Koselleck, eds., *Geschichtliche Grundbegriffe: Historisches Lexikon zur politisch–sozialen Sprache in Deutschland* (vol. 6, 323–444). Stuttgart: Klett-Cotta, 1990.

Walzer, Michael. *Just and Unjust Wars: A Moral Argument with Historical Illustrations* (4th edn.). New York: Basic Books, 2015.

Warrick, Joby. *Black Flags: The Rise of ISIS*. New York: Anchor Books, 2016.

Wieviorka, Michel. *The Making of Terrorism*. Translated by David Gordon White. Chicago, IL: University of Chicago Press, 1993.

Wieviorka, Michel. *Violence: A New Approach*. Translated by David Macey. London: SAGE, 2005.

Zafirovski, Milan, and Daniel G. Rodeheaver, eds. *Modernity and Terrorism: From Anti-Modernity to Modern Global Terror*. Chicago, IL: Haymarket Books, 2014.

Zineb el Rhazoui. *13: Zineb raconte l'enfer du 13 novembre avec 13 témoins au coeur des attaques*. Paris: Ring, 2016.

Žižek, Slavoj. *Blasphemische Gedanken: Islam und Moderne*. Berlin: Ullstein Verlag, 2016.

Žižek, Slavoj. *The New Class Struggle: The Real Reasons for Flight and Terror*. Translated by Regina Schneider. Berlin: Ullstein Verlag, 2015.

Žižek, Slavoj. *Slavoj Žižek Presents Trotsky: Terrorism and Communism*. London: Verso, 2017.

Žižek, Slavoj. *Welcome to the Desert of the Real: Five Essays on September 11 and Related Dates*. London: Verso, 2013.